Imag

MW01156001

305

IMAGINATION
in Teaching and Learning

THE MIDDLE SCHOOL YEARS

Kieran Egan

The University of Chicago Press

Kieran Egan is professor of education at Simon Fraser University in British Columbia. His work on imagination has earned him the 1991 Grawemeyer Award for Education and he is the author or editor of seven books including *Teaching as Story Telling*, the latter published by the University of Chicago Press.

The University of Chicago Press, Chicago 60637
The Althouse Press, London, Ontario, Canada
in association with Routledge, London

Printed in Canada

01 00 99 98 97 96 95 94 93 92   6 5 4 3 2 1

ISBN: 0-226-19033-1 (cloth); 0-226-19035-8 (paper)

Library of Congress Cataloguing-in-Publication Data

Egan, Kieran.
    Imagination in teaching and learning : the middle school years / Kieran Egan.
        p.   cm.
    Includes index.

    1. Teaching. 2. Imagination in children. 3. Storytelling.
    4. Middle schools--Curricula.   I. Title.
    LB1027.E413   1992   91-45085
    373.11'02--dc20   CIP

This book is printed on acid-free paper.

To Susanna, with love

CONTENTS

Acknowledgements i
Introduction 1

I A Very Short History of the Imagination 9

Introduction 9
Myth, Memory, and Emotion 10
Ancient and Medieval Imagination 12
Imagination in the Enlightenment 18
The Romantic Imagination 22
Imagination in the Modern Period:
    Philosophical Work 26
Imagination in the Modern Period:
    Psychological Work 33
Conclusion 36

II Why Is Imagination Important to Education? 45

Introduction 45
Imagination and Conventional Thinking 46
Imagination in Learning 49
Imagination and Memory 52
Social Virtues 54
Imagination and Freedom 57
Imagination and Objective Knowledge 59
Vizualization, Originality, and Creativity 61
The Narrative Mind 62
Conclusion 65

III Characteristics of Students' Imaginative Lives,
    Ages 8-15 67

Introduction 67
The Affective Connection 69
Extremes and Limits 72
Romance, Wonder, and Awe 75
Associating With the Heroic 80

Revolt and Idealism 82
Matters of Detail 84
Humanizing Knowledge 86
Conclusion 88

IV **Imagination and Teaching** 91

Introduction 91
A Planning Framework For
    Imaginative Teaching and Learning 93
Exploration of the Framework by
    Means of an Example 93
Less Formal Implementations:
    Fragmenting the Framework 102
From Characteristics to Principles of Learning 107
Conclusion 112

V **Image and Concept** 115

VI **Some Further Examples** 119

Introduction 119
Mathematics 120
Science 125
Social Studies 133
Language Arts 144
Conclusion 151

Conclusion 153

The Role of the Teacher 154
The Imaginative Curriculum 156
Eliminating Social Studies and Humanities 159
Imagination and Entertainment 162
Interests and Abilities: Educational Clichés 163
The Moral Dimension 165
The Logic of the Heart 166

References 169
Index 175

Acknowledgements

I am most grateful for the help of those teachers who have given me suggestions, criticism, and advice, and who have adopted and adapted in their practice various of the ideas in this book. In particular I am grateful to Miranda Armstrong, Ann Connolly, and Kathy Saville of Eltham College, Melbourne, and to Di Fleming of Methodist Ladies College, Melbourne, to Sandy Chamberlain and the late, greatly missed, June Ciba, and teachers at Maple Lane, Lord Byng, and Westwind schools in Richmond, British Columbia, to Pierre Blouin and Scott Seyer from Surrey, British Columbia, to Tim Watson at King Edward VII School, Worcester, England, and to those teachers who enrolled in various offerings of "Imagination in teaching and learning" at Simon Fraser University. Colleagues at Simon Fraser who have kindly given their time and comments on drafts of this book include Sharon Bailin, Robin Barrow, Roger Gehlbach, David Hammond, Geoff Madoc-Jones, and Stuart Richmond. The book is better for their helpful criticisms. Maria do Céu Roldão, Escola Superior de Educacão, Portalegre, Portugal, Don Gutteridge and Geoff Milburn, University of Western Ontario, Brian Sutton-Smith, John Willinsky, University of British Columbia, and John Wilson, University of Oxford, have also improved the book by their generously given comments. I am indebted also to the insightful and challenging criticisms made on the manuscript by the publisher's reviewers. Parts of Chapter Two appeared as an article in the *Harvard Educational Review*, and I am grateful to its editors and publisher for permission to reprint it here. Eileen Mallory has 'processed' the manuscript through various drafts with her usual supernatural speed and accuracy, and the good cheer with which she has done so leaves me always grateful. During the writing of this book I was the grateful recipient of a research grant from the Social Sciences and Humanities Research Council of Canada.

Introduction

It seems generally agreed that imagination is a good thing and that it ought to be stimulated and developed in education. Two related obstacles stand in the way of our routinely achieving this; first, it is difficult to get a clear grasp on what imagination is, and, second, whatever it is, it does not seem the kind of thing that lends itself to practical methods and techniques that any teacher can easily employ in classroom instruction. The purpose of this book is to try to make a little headway against both of these obstacles. I want to combine a more articulate grasp on imagination with the normal requirements and constraints of classroom teaching and learning, to come up with some practical help for the teacher who wants to engage, stimulate, and develop students' imaginations.

When talking with students, teachers, educational administrators, or professors of education about good teachers, it is very common to hear teachers commended as "imaginative". The kinds of things they do in class are frequently — to use Barrow's (1990) joint criteria for imaginativeness — unusual and effective. Such teachers show a flexibility of mind that enables them to present a subject in a new and engaging way, a way that enables students to understand it better and also to take pleasure from the learning. Given the frequency with which, in informal discussion, imagination is identified as a crucial feature of good teaching, it is surprising to find it almost totally ignored in research on teaching effectiveness. (In a review of such research, O'Neil [1988] identifies twenty "research factors", but "imagination" is not among them. Similarly, Porter and Brophy's [1988] review and synthesis of research on "good teaching" also ignores imagination.) This is no doubt in part due to the difficulty dominant research methods have in coming to grips with imagination, but it would be a great pity if its virtual absence in empirical research should encourage us to focus on the kinds of behavioural repertoires prominent in that research and ignore something so obviously central to good teaching as imagination. There is something in this of the old joke about looking for a lost key on the clean pavement under the bright street lamp because it is easy to see there, even though the key was dropped in the long grass further down the street where there is no light. Even though this book may occasionally seem to be feeling its way through tangles, it is at least, I think, looking in the right place for keys to effective teaching.

This book, then, is not about unusually imaginative students and teachers. Rather, my focus is on the characteristics of the typical student's imaginative life and how this can be engaged in learning, and on how the typical teacher might plan lessons and units to achieve this aim, and on how the typical curriculum content of science, social studies, language arts, mathematics, and so on, might be shaped also to help achieve this aim.

Mary Warnock, in her study of imagination (1976), asserted that "the cultivation of imagination...should be the chief aim of education" (p. 9), and that "we have a duty to educate the imagination above all else" (p. 10). We might reasonably feel wary of such bold claims. Though perhaps we need to say first, "It depends what you mean by 'imagination'". It will be obvious that I think it is important to cultivate the imagination, but one of the reasons I have some reluctance in agreeing wholeheartedly with Warnock has to do with the persisting difficulty, despite her admirable work and that of others I will draw on in this book, of getting clear about what imagination is, or about the range of things the word is used to cover. We can begin by observing that people, even those who have been most intimately involved in studying it and promoting its value in education, mean rather different things by the term.

This variety in the meanings of imagination was brought home to me a few years ago when I co-edited with Dan Nadaner a book entitled *Imagination and education* (1988). Dan and I were delighted with the quality of the essays we were able to solicit from so many outstanding educational writers, including Robin Barrow, Maxine Greene, poet laureate Ted Hughes, Gareth Matthews, Roger Shepard, Brian Sutton-Smith, and many others. But when it came to organizing the set of essays, we faced unexpected problems. Central was the fact that many of our authors clearly conceived of the imagination rather differently. Indeed, one would be hard put to show that any two (including the editors' contributions) meant quite the same thing by imagination.

And yet we all use the word fairly confidently; confident, that is, about more or less what we mean and that what we mean will be understood by others as what they more or less mean by the word. I think this confidence is not misplaced. That is, we use "imagination" to refer to a range of capacities we share. There is, I suspect, a fair amount of intuitive agreement about what this range involves. Once we try to excavate it, and categorize it, and label the parts, however, we seem to create disagreements or, at least, dissatisfaction with the characterizations. The problem seems to lie in the complex and protean nature of imagination, and in the fact that imagination lies at the crux of those aspects of our lives that are least well understood.

When people try to describe the imagination, most frequently they refer to the capacity we have in common to hold images in our minds of what may not be present or even exist, and sometimes to allow these images to affect us as though they were present and real. The nature of these images is very hard for us to describe, as they are unlike any other kinds of images we are familiar with in the "external" world. It seems, also, that people experience these images quite differently — some having clear access to vivid quasi-pictorial images, some having such hazy experiences that the word "image" seems not appropriate. And the same person may be familiar with this range of what seem like different kinds or degrees of "images".

Imagination lies at a kind of crux where perception, memory, idea generation, emotion, metaphor, and no doubt other labelled features of our lives, intersect and interact. Some of the images we experience seem "echoes" of what we have perceived, though we can change them, combine them, manipulate them to become like nothing we have ever perceived. Our memory seems to be able to transform perceptions and store their "echoes" in ways that do not always or perhaps very often require quasi-pictorial "images", (as in the cases of sounds and smells, say). Novelty in ideas has nearly always been connected with the powers of imagination to "see" solutions to problems. Our emotions seem tied to these mental images; when we imagine something we tend to *feel* as though it is real or present, such that it seems our "coding" and "access" to images is tied in with our emotions. The logic of imagination seems to conform more readily with that of metaphor than with any scheme of rationality we can be explicit about.

Most of these observations about the imagination, which one finds in the literature on the topic, tend to draw on the obvious connection between imagination and imagery. But we also "talk quite properly of imagining reasons, differences, dilemmas and lies, of imaginary wants and happiness, of imaginable caution and torment, of imagining what, why and how, and of imagining that, e.g., we believe so-and-so, that we can do such-and-such....Yet none of this is imageable" (White, 1990, p. 6). By recognizing that our everyday use of "imagination" refers, perhaps most often, to the non-pictorial and non-imageable, we realize that the imagination is not simply a capacity to form images, but is a capacity to think in a particular way. It is a way that crucially involves our capacity to think of the possible rather than just the actual.

In Chapter One, then, I will try to give a brief account of the range of meanings people have ascribed to "imagination". As our current complex concept is in significant part a product of past uses, I will try, as it were, to unroll the senses of imagination that have rolled together through the centuries. I will try to be as explicit as I can about the sense of imagination that we use today with some confidence of being understood, of partaking in a shared meaning. I will then use that "more articulate grasp" through the rest of the book to work on imagination in education.

This historical and theoretical chapter seems to me appropriate in what is intended as a practice-oriented book, because of the common imprecision that has accompanied discussion of imagination in education. I think a more explicit and clearer conception should help one to apply the ideas from the rest of the book. But I do recognize that such an introduction might seem unnecessary or redundant to some readers whose primary interest is in the book's main practical purpose. That is, I think one can simply accept the generally prevailing, intuitive sense of imagination and one can read and make sense of the book beginning with Chapter Two, but that working through Chapter One should prove worthwhile for later practice.

In Chapter Two I will consider why it is important to stimulate and develop the imagination if one hopes to educate. I will begin with general claims such as those of Warnock cited above, and John Dewey's: "The imagination is the medium of appreciation in every field" (1966, p. 236). I will use the articulated conception of imagination from Chapter One to refine these observations, not to disagree with them but rather to move them to a point where we can see more clearly *what to do* in order to stimulate and develop imagination in teaching. So much of the focus on students' cognition is in terms of logico-mathematical skills that our very concept of education becomes affected. I hope that by taking the imagination more seriously in education a more proportionate concept might be encouraged.

Chapter Three will focus on learning, and in particular on those characteristics of typical students' imaginations that can be used to aid more meaningful learning. I will try to outline prominent characteristics of students' imaginative lives in order to see how we might design learning activities that engage the imagination. There is very little research to draw on here, and I will provide what might rather grandly be called an analysis of ethnographic studies of the materials and activities in which students' imaginative activity is most intensely engaged.

In Chapter Four I will draw on the previous chapters, especially Chapter Three, to design a framework or model for planning teaching that aims to stimulate students' imaginations. I will begin with a fairly comprehensive framework and describe it by showing an example of its use in planning a unit of study. Thereafter I will consider less formal ways in which teachers might draw on the characterization of students' imaginative lives in order to plan more engaging lessons and units.

Chapter Five is intended very briefly to emphasize the usefulness of forming and articulating vivid images in teaching. So much educational literature, encouraged no doubt by the consistent focus on logico-mathematical forms of thinking, emphasizes the development and use of concepts that it sometimes seems the educational uses of images is often neglected.

In the final chapter I will give examples of how the framework can be used to plan teaching in a variety of curriculum areas. I will try to show how one might use the principles articulated earlier in the book to teach in an imaginatively stimulating way such topics as the geometrical theorem that parallel lines cut by a transversal form congruent alternate interior angles, and a science/environmental unit on trees, and a social studies unit on government, and a language arts unit on mythology. Along with the example in Chapter Four, which is on eels, I try to show how the framework and the principles it embodies can be put into practice in different curriculum areas.

While the focus of this book is on students' imaginative lives, this is a teacher-centred book. This does not mean that it seeks to depreciate the value of student activity, initiative, or construction in their learning. Nor does it seek to suggest that the classroom should be made up of active, energetic teachers dominating passive students, or anything like that. Far from it. Rather, it is teacher-centred simply in the sense of being a book designed for teachers, and it will be looking at the classroom and students' learning and imagination from a teachers' viewpoint. If I emphasize teaching and planning for teaching, and so on, this is not to imply that I consider no other activity has a proper place in the classroom.

The subtitle refers to the middle school years. I mean middle school rather generously, intending this book to be of use to teachers of students from about ages eight to fifteen. I recognize that this is rather an odd age-range for an educational text, given the enormous changes of adolescence and the fact that virtually all psychological theories etch significant stage divisions within this period. We do not have any developmental theories that focus on the imagination. But if we reflect for a moment on the typical range and forms of imaginative activity in childhood, youth, and maturity, there is little to suggest that such a theory would readily parallel those developmental theories that focus primarily on logico-mathematical intellectual activity. The typically progressive, "hierarchical integrative" form of psychological theories of development seems, on the face of it, not likely to capture adequately what we may informally observe about the changing character of imaginative life as people grow older. So, while the age eight-to-fifteen period does not fit easily with current psychological theories or the administrative arrangements of schooling, I think there are sufficient similarities in the forms of imaginative life during these years to justify, and even require, treating this age-range together.

As I try to characterize prominent features of students' imaginations in Chapter Three, I hope teachers familiar with this age-range will recognize them as indeed accurate: will recognize that their students do indeed exhibit these characteristics. This should be the case, as the characterizations have been derived from a study of the materials, books, games, T.V. shows, songs, films, and experiences that students typically find most imaginatively engaging in this period. In this short book, designed primarily to be of some practical help to teachers, there is not the space to provide the extensive theoretical support for my claim about the appropriateness of dealing with this age-range together, nor to do more than cite examples to support my characterization of students' imaginative lives. But perhaps I might mention that this book, while intended to be sufficient in itself to the aims of providing a more articulate grasp on imagination and practical methods for stimulating and developing students' imaginations, is a part of a larger project. Among the purposes of this larger project is to supply what I noted above as lacking: a developmental theory that focusses on the imagination. If you wish to follow up the topic of this book in greater detail, or consider related ideas on imagination and learning among younger children, other books in this project might be of interest.

This book is, as it were, vertically related to *Teaching as story telling* (Egan, 1986), which tries to do a similar job for younger children — up to about age eight. It is, as it were, horizontally related to *Romantic understanding: The development of rationality and imagination, ages 8 to 15* (Egan, 1990), which deals with a much wider range of students' "sense-making capacities" and looks at them in much greater detail than is possible here. In this latter book may be found the grounds to support treating the eight-to-fifteen age-range together, along with a much fuller theoretical and empirical support for the characterization of students' imaginative lives. (*Teaching as story telling* is similarly related to *Primary Understanding: Education in early childhood* [Egan, 1988].) *Teaching as story telling* and this book are designed primarily to take some of the central ideas related to students' imaginative development from the larger and more theoretical works, focus on their practical implications, and move in the direction of techniques that teachers can add to their set of professional skills.

CHAPTER ONE

A Very Short History of Imagination

Introduction

The point of trying to sketch even a *very* short history of imagination is due to the way such a complex concept accumulates its meaning. What we mean by the term today is a compound of residues of various meanings people have had of it in the past. Many of our most complex concepts are accumulations of meanings whose constituents often do not always entirely cohere. We have a sense of vagueness about such concepts. In the case of imagination, I think this sense of vagueness is due in part to its complexity but also in part to its containing a number of elements that do not sit comfortably together. I think we can clarify its present complex meaning by unfolding some of the ideas that have folded into it over the centuries.

The old style of intellectual history — in which modern Western thought is taken as an unequivocal pinnacle reached by a progressive, evolutionary path from the confusions of myth, through the glories of Greece and Rome, the Renaissance, Enlightenment, and so on, to ourselves in the present — has hit a number of snags of late. This is a particularly unhelpful paradigm or story-line if our focus is imagination. In as far as imagination is assumed generally to be a good thing, it is far from clear that it is more fully exercised, more evidently life-enhancing, more socially beneficial now than at the beginnings of human history. We have difficulty denying that in the mythologies of the world there is evidence of imaginative life of a vivid power rarely encountered in the Western intellectual tradition today.

So let us begin with imagination in mythic cultures, and then try to trace something of its career in the mental life of the West. In the conclusion to this chapter, I will synthesize as well as I can the persistent features evident in the varied uses of the concept, trying to provide that "more articulate grasp" on imagination.

Myth, Memory, and Emotion

Whatever scholars have made of myth — which has not been much until quite recently — all have had to acknowledge that in its varied forms it certainly exemplifies imaginative activity. Some used to argue that it is the kind of crazy thinking that results from the imagination running wild, without the constraints of rationality. As such, it was claimed to be unproductive thought, reasonless, like the unconscious rambling of a demented dreamer (cf. Blumenberg, 1985; Kirk, 1970). And yet it is ubiquitous in oral cultures.

Why do we find such vivid and powerful imaginative thought at the earliest times from which we have any traces? The closeness to oral myth is commonly assumed to be responsible for the power of the earliest Western literature, of Homer and the epic poets of the near-East and Scandinavia, of the Indian Vedas, of Aeschylus and Sophocles, and so on. Myth, it is increasingly clear, is evidence of great intellectual energy, not of some infirmity of the mind.

Perhaps we may pose our question another way: What social needs were fulfilled by such highly developed imaginative activity so early in human cultural history? The simple answer seems to be that this imaginative vividness was stimulated by the need to remember. In oral cultures, people know only what they can remember. The lore that binds a tribe together, and helps to establish each individual's social roles and very sense of identity, is coded into the myths. The myths are held to be sacred, and they are passed on with the utmost care. They contain the divine warrant for the social arrangements that give the tribe its structure and character; they determine appropriate marriage partners, appropriate behaviour and feelings towards relations and others within the tribe, appropriate economic activities, and so on.

Why cannot this lore be preserved in some more straight-forward or systematic or — we would be tempted to say — rational form? Why are not explicit directions or lists of activities, regulations and laws preserved? The answer seems to be twofold: first, such lists or explicit directions would be very hard to remember faithfully through many generations and, second, they would not attract people's emotional commitment to them.

The amount of lore or "information" contained in a corpus of myths is quite considerable, and recent research has confirmed what myth-users knew long ago — that we can remember a set of vivid events plotted into a story much better than we can remember lists or sets of explicit directions. The second point is related to this but, while no less important, is perhaps more complex. The great power of the story is that it engages us affectively as well as requiring our cognitive attention; we learn the content of the story while we are emotionally engaged by its characters or events.

The vividness and power of myth stories turns on the way we are arrested by their images. They are typically strange and unlike anything in our experience or environment. It was discovered long ago that the more vivid the images used to encode a tribe's lore, the more easily and securely it was remembered. This discovery has been the basis of all memorizing techniques developed in the pre-historic, medieval, and modern worlds. Those advertisements which promise to "Improve your memory in 30 days!" are based, usually rather inefficiently, on techniques that were already ancient thousands of years ago, and which reached a second peak of development in the Middle Ages (Spence, 1984; Yates, 1966).

So it was the need to memorize things that early stimulated and developed the human capacity for imagination. Patterning of sound, vivid images, and story structuring were, we might sensibly observe, the most important early social inventions. It was these technical linguistic tools, and their effects on the mind, that helped human groups to cohere and remain relatively stable.

These techniques do not become irrelevant after the invention of writing, of course. Patterned sound, vivid images, and stories continue today to do important work for us. In this first stage of our very short history of imagination, however, we should note the close connections, discovered early, among imagination and memory and emotion. Such connections are recognized in the Greek myths, where Mnemosyne, goddess of memory, is mother to the Muses, the goddesses of poetry, literature, music, dance, and so on. (The "and so on" included in later antiquity all intellectual pursuits. Plato and Aristotle organized their schools as associations for the cult of the Muses. Thus Museum came to mean a place of education and research.) Imagination and memory have seemed to many people throughout history to be closely allied; both can call ideas or images into our minds, and those of imagination, while they have a freedom memory lacks, seem to rely on memory to supply their raw materials.

Ancient and Medieval Imagination

As the tower of Babel grew ever higher towards heaven, the Hebrew Jehovah said "Behold the people, how nothing will be restrained from them, from what they have imagined to do" (Genesis: II, 6). The beginning of human history as described in the book of Genesis involves a similar act in which the first people encroach on God's prerogatives. Adam and Eve eat the fruit of the tree of the knowledge of good and evil so that they might have divine knowledge. That act heralds the beginning of history, in which people can remember a past and imagine a future different from the present. They can form plans, that is, for conditions that are presently non-existent.

The main Hebrew term for imagination is "yetser", whose root is the same as that of "yetsirah", which we translate as "creation". In both of the above stories, human beings are trespassing on powers that properly belong to God. That people are to remember this and desist from so doing is made clear by the punishments visited on Adam and Eve and on the builders of Babel. In both cases, acts of rebellion against the limits God set for human beings exhibit the power to imagine a future that is different from the past. But, as Kearney puts it: "As a power first dramatized in man's defiance of divine prohibition, the *yetser* bears the stigma of a stolen possession" (1988, pp. 40/41).

Throughout the ancient Hebrew tradition, the *yetser* is considered a dangerous capacity. It seems inescapably bound up with attempts to usurp God's creative power. Human creativity, that product of the active imagination, is seen constantly threatening to divide God from His people. The attempt to imagine what is not given human beings to know is the source of our difficulties; that is a persistent message of the Talmud. So Moses brings the commandment against trying to make any image of God, who is unknowable and unrepresentable.

The ancient Greek myth of Prometheus tells a similar story. Prometheus steals fire from the gods and gives it to humans. The power over fire enables human beings to transform their world and to encroach on the prerogatives of the gods. Prometheus suffers an even nastier fate than did Adam and Eve. Pro-metheus means fore-thinker; one with the power to see or imagine a different future:

> Above all Prometheus made possible the imaginative en-hancement of experience, the...distinction between what happens to us and what we make of this happening....The imagination has always been a contentious power, as a result, so far as men are concerned in their relations with the gods. (Donoghue, 1973, p. 26)

The imagination in both ancient Greek and Hebrew traditions represents a rebellion against divine order, it disturbs the proper harmony between the human and the divine worlds, and it empowers people with a capacity that is properly divine. The main sense of imagination in both these traditions, however, is more like what we mean by foresight or planning. The creative element which looms so large in modern conceptions is in the ancient world only dimly glimpsed and hinted at in a disturbed way; creativity remains a prerogative of the divine. It is the power to make a world, perform miracles, destroy cities, cause earthquakes. This kind of power, and the imagination that frames it, is beyond the capacities that humans can deploy.

In the classical Greek world the sense of imagination is elaborated, particularly in the work of Plato. His ideas exerted an immense influence for two thousand years, the wake of which still pulls hard at us. Plato articulated an image of human life and education that placed the highest value on the development of reason. Reason was of value because through its use one could gain secure knowledge about what was real and true about the world and about experience. One distinction which he bequeathed to Western culture was between this reasoning faculty that can know the truth and the faculty of imagination that can only *mimic* the appearance of things. In Plato's view, painting and poetry are not among the greatest expressions of creative power, but rather are inferior activities, caught up with appearances and unable to move towards abstract ideas through which alone truth may be approached. In his dialogue, *Protagoras*, Plato sees Prometheus's theft as not simply of fire but of the cultural arts of making things with it. All imaginative acts, all making of images, however, are simply copies of the original creative acts of the gods. As the original is the reality we live among, then all copies must be inadequate and false in one way or another. Such images are particularly deceptive says Plato, echoing Moses, because they may "misrepresent the nature of gods" (*Republic* [Cornford, p. 69]).

The original *idea* of a bed is what we must know in order to be able to recognize something as a bed. What the carpenter makes is, then, one remove from that ultimate reality; it is merely an example, a more or less inadequate attempt, to give practical shape to the ideal bed. But the painter who makes an image of that bed is twice removed from reality. The painter is just copying the carpenter's copy. The painter is ignorant of everything about the bed except how it looks. Art, then, can teach us nothing about what is true and real.

This perhaps seems odd to us today. We no doubt go along with Plato about the importance of trying to discover what is real and true about the world and experience. But we tend to think that what is real and true is indeed in the world accessible to our senses, not in some world of ideal abstractions. Well, obviously, this is hardly to do justice to the complexity of Plato's ideas about knowledge, but it suggests that his conception of imagination and its functions is not one in which they are highly valued. Indeed he sees images as appealing to the lower parts of our nature and strengthening the lower functions of our minds at the expense of the higher. So those activities which might stimulate and develop the imagination have tended to get short shrift in educational schemes influenced by Plato's ideas — which pretty well includes all those of the Western world. The Platonic emphasis is on a curriculum of gradually accumulating and clarifying forms of knowledge.

There has, of course, always been retained some degree of interest in developing the imagination. A rather different valuation of imagination is evident in the influential work of one of Plato's students. Aristotle argued — against Plato — that the artistic imagination is not simply portraying copies of copies of things. Rather the artist tries to represent universal features of human experience; the aim is not simply copying, but rather showing through the particulars something more generally true about the world.

Aristotle considered mental images to be the way we connect our sensations of the world with our reason. So to Aristotle the imagination is constantly involved in our intellectual activity: "Every time one thinks one must at the same time contemplate some image" (*De Anima*, 432a). Aristotle prefigures ideas that we will see more fully developed during the Enlightenment and Romantic periods. But seeing the imagination as something that plays a constant role in perception makes it a potential contributor to rational thought rather than the Platonic deceiver and seducer of the mind away from rationality.

But in Aristotle's work, as well as in Plato's, the imagination is still a faculty that copies what is in the world. It is dependent on the sensations or on reason: "Imagination remains largely a *reproductive* rather than a *productive* activity, a servant rather than a master of meaning, imitation rather than origin" (Kearney, 1988, p. 113); or, as Croce puts it:

> Ancient psychology knew fancy or imagination as a faculty
> midway between sense and intellect, but always as conservative

and reproductive of sensuous impressions or conveying conceptions to the senses, never properly as a productive autonomous activity. (1972, p. 170)

It is difficult to be entirely precise about Plato's and Aristotle's sense of imagination, however, because their Greek did not have an exact equivalent for the English word. *Phantasma* is the closest term that most commonly overlaps with what we refer to as "imagination". But it has a more general sense of "appearance" or "how things appear". *Phantasmata*, for example, are involved in phenomena like the sun appearing small, in such illusions as the land appearing to move when we are on board ship, in delusions during illness, and in instances where we allow irrational passions to make things appear to us as we wish them rather than as they are. Not all of these are cases where we would today readily use "imagination". On the whole, unlike Plato, Aristotle "lays little stress on its [phantasma] use to envisage possibilities other than the actual. More prominence is given to the passive reception of appearances than to the active power to call them up" (White, 1990, p. 9).

During the Medieval period we find no significantly different conceptions of the imagination from those inherited from the ancient Hebrew and Greek traditions. At the beginning of the Middle Ages or at the end of the Roman Empire — depending on how you see St. Augustine's (354-430) work — we find "imaginatio" used in a way that combines the Biblical distrust of images with the Platonic sense of them as a hindrance to philosophical contemplation. For St. Augustine they were additionally a threat to spiritual life. Imagination is considered at best a somewhat distrusted servant of higher intellectual functions. During the later Middle Ages, St. Bonaventure (c. 1217-1274) accepts that the imagination can be useful if it carries the mind towards God, but he emphasizes that it must be kept firmly under the control of reason or it will more likely lead in the other direction. For those in whom reason is not highly developed, imagination is also likely to lead people to take images for what they are merely images of.

St. Thomas Aquinas, profoundly influenced by Aristotle, considers the imagination a kind of mediator between mind and body; it passes up to the reason in the form of images what it takes from perception, and the intellect then purifies these images into abstract ideas. But, despite this role in thinking, the imagination is still to be distrusted as a particularly weak part of the mind, susceptible to confusing its images with reality — or to being induced to do so: "Demons are known to work on men's imagination, until everything is other than it is" (Aquinas, *Summa Theologica*, 5, 147).

That, anyway, is the official church conception of imagination, preserved in philosophical texts. Less accessible, however, is the rather different view embodied in uses of the profane imagination in popular culture. In this intellectual underworld it would appear to have been celebrated and enjoyed in witchcraft, folklore, occultism, and other realms where the body, dreams and magic enjoyed an energetic currency denied them by the church (Le Goff, 1986).

But prior to the Enlightenment it must be said that the imagination was not considered either particularly interesting or energetic in our mental lives. This lack of enthusiasm seems a result of the conclusion that the imagination was almost entirely a *mimetic* faculty — it copies reality or draws its images from perception. The fact that it can create images of things never seen could be easily accommodated to this mimetic conception. You form an image of a horse; you form an image of wings; you imagine the wings stuck on the horse; and so you imagine a flying horse — to use Thomas Hobbes's example (1962, p. 3). Or as Plato puts it:

> Imagine...the figure of a multifarious and many-headed beast, girt
> · round with heads of animals, tame and wild, which it can grow
> out of itself and transform at will. That would tax the skill of a
> sculptor; but luckily the stuff of imagination is easier to mould
> than wax. (*Republic* [Cornford, p. 316])

Why make a fuss about such a commonplace capacity? The fuss might better be directed at the use made of it. Plato's concerns were echoed in a different context when the Inquisitor of Toledo condemned El Greco's religious paintings: "I like neither the angels you paint nor the saints. Instead of making people pray, they make them admire. Beauty inserts itself as an obstacle between our souls and God" (cited in Kearney, 1988, p. 10).

The persisting influences of Plato and Aristotle are evident in Pico della Mirandola's treatise *On the Imagination* composed at the beginning of the sixteenth century. We find, somewhat debased, such Platonic sentiments as: "Imagination conforms with intellect, in being free, unfixed, and devoted to no special object. But it is surpassed by intellect, since it conceives and fashions the sensible and particular only, while intellect, in addition, conceives and fashions the universal and intelligible, and such things as are purified from all contact with matter" (1930, p. 33). Similarly Platonic is his admonition: "We must strive with all our powers to the end that everwatchful reason may incessantly stand guard before the gates of the mind, that it may repel those phantoms which refuse to obey it" (1930, p. 79). But we also find fairly straightforward echoes from Aristotle's *De Anima*: we are told that imagination "enters into alliance with" all superior intellectual powers, which could not function unless imagination "support and assist them" (1930, p. 33) and that "imagination itself is midway between incorporeal and corporeal nature, and is the medium through which they are joined" (1930, p. 37).

Another reason for the lack of fuss about this commonplace capacity was due to the more profound and meaningful experiences that we today associate with imagination being then associated with the concept of the soul. But once the centrality of the soul to people's conceptions of themselves began to wane, so imagination began to "grow" into the place it vacated (McFarland, 1985).

Imagination in the Enlightenment

René Descartes (1596-1650), early in the Enlightenment, reasserted a conception of the mind as properly governed by reason, and of analytical reason as adequate to properly make sense of experience and the cosmos. So he concluded: "This power of imagination which I possess is in no way necessary to my essence...for although I did not possess it I should still remain the same that I now am" (1917, p. 127). Descartes also wrote of "the misleading judgement that proceeds from the blundering constructions of the imagination" (1931, p. 7). In all his references to the imagination, it is clear that his conception of it was limited to, dependent on, and equivalent to the forming of images (White, 1990, Ch. 3). His student, Nicholas Malebranche (1638-1715), wrote a treatise called *The Search for Truth*, which describes the senses, the imagination, and the passions as obstacles to be overcome by reason in *its* search for truth. Clearly the imagination had no significant part to play in this search.

This aggressive rationalism, along with the beginnings of modern scientific inquiry during the same period, had no need for a sense of the imagination as anything other than the mimetic and ornamental faculty of the ancient and medieval worlds. Francis Bacon observed that imagination "hardly produces sciences" but only poetry or art, which is "to be accounted rather as a pleasure or play of wit than a science" (1864-74, Vol. 4, p. 406). This rationalism was not without its critics, however. And it is in their work that we see the gradual expansion of imagination from a kind of ornamental, entertaining, *mimetic* faculty into a centre and source of meaning and originality in human experience.

But that expansion was slow. Early in the eighteenth century Addison concluded his series of pieces on the imagination by observing that: "The pleasures of the imagination, taken in their full extent, are not so gross as those of sense, nor so refined as those of the understanding" (*The Spectator*, Monday, June 23rd, 1712). Addison clearly thinks that the imagination is not a serious part of the mind's equipment, but rather that it adds a kind of ornamental delight or "bestows charms" or offers "a kind of refreshment" to the serious and hard-working understanding and reason. This is a sense of imagination that equates it very largely with "fancy" — a kind of idle, frothy, mind-wandering entertainment.

Key to associating imagination with the centres of creativity and meaning is the separation of fancy and imagination, and the allotting to fancy those *mimetic*, ornamental, charming activities, and to imagination many of the faculties earlier associated with the soul, along with some other new ones (Engell, 1982). But the classical view of imagination as primarily a kind of intermediary between sense perception and reason persisted until the latter part of the eighteenth century, and while attention was increasingly given to its powers of novelty, these were still distinguished from whatever generated ideas within us:

> Besides the ideas...which are presented to the senses; the mind of man possesses a sort of creative power of its own; either in representing at pleasure the images of things in the order and manner in which they are received by the senses, or in combining those images in a new manner, and according to a different order. This power is called Imagination; and to this belongs whatever is called wit, fancy, invention and the like. But it must be observed, that this power of the imagination is incapable of producing anything absolutely new; it can only vary the disposition of those ideas which it has received from the senses. (Burke [1757], 1967, pp. 16,17)

Even as Burke propounded what was the advanced, educated view of the time, the Scottish philosopher David Hume (1711-76) continued to publish his revolutionary ideas to a largely indifferent world. Indeed, for twenty years preceding Burke's account of imagination, Hume had been writing and publishing work which laid the basis for a revolution in philosophy and psychology. Hume had initially expected enthusiastic applause, furious attacks, and through it all detailed scholarly scrutiny and controversy, for which he was prepared. Instead, his ideas were generally neglected, or were read with bewilderment, and the few who bothered to respond did so with dismissive scorn. But one of his readers understood him. The German philosopher, Immanuel Kant (1724-1804), followed up Hume's work, which led, among much else, to a significantly changed conception of the nature and function of the imagination.

Hume distinguished between "impressions", which are what we are aware of in perception, and "ideas", which are images of these impressions which we form in the mind. This image-forming faculty plays, so far, much the same role between sense and reason conceived for it earlier. But Hume also argued that our perception of the world is fleeting, partial, constantly changing, and yet what is delivered to the mind is a stable, clear, constant image of the world. How is the latter stable and constant image generated from the flux of perceptions? Hume, who was very much a hard-nosed empiricist, reluctantly concluded that this crucial role at the very foundation of our mind's functioning was performed by the imagination.

Kant went even further. He could not accept Hume's notion that what we actually perceive are discontinuous and partial "impressions". Kant argues that "impressions" are perceived as already organized and structured. So we do not need to see the imagination as somehow creating coherent images out of incoherent perceptions. Rather imagination is pushed, as it were, to perform the even more fundamental task of providing the prior structuring of our perceptions. That is, what we *can* perceive, and know, is predetermined by our imagination. What we experience is the world already structured by the imagination. So, at the most basic level of meaning-making, the imagination is active.

Both Hume and Kant associate a number of other qualities with imagination, qualities that have affected our modern conception of it. Hume, for example, notes the connection between imagination and our feelings: "Lively passions commonly attend a lively imagination" ([1739] 1888, p. 427). He notes further that: "It is remarkable that the imagination and affections have a close union together, and that nothing which affects the former can be entirely indifferent to the latter" ([1739] 1888, p. 424). Kant observes that the imagination can generate in us ideas that cannot be expressed or represented in any other form; ideas of infinite space, endless numbers, eternal duration can also fill us with complex emotions involving wonder and the sense of the sublime. But what is sublime is only secondarily the intangible features of the cosmos: "What is sublime is our own minds in contemplating them" (Warnock, 1976, p. 63). So attention inward to the wonder of the mind itself comes along with the new conception of imagination. There is a world within, no less interesting and open for exploration as the world outside.

"The imagination is a powerful agent for creating as it were a second nature out of the material supplied to it by actual nature" (Kant, [1790] 1952, p. 314). Here is a different imagination from that of the classical world. It is proclaimed as central to our sense-making but yet is ineffable even to those who gave it its modern shape; it is, to Hume, "a kind of magical faculty of the soul" (1888, p. 24). Herder, influenced by Kant, says in the late 1780s:

> Of all the powers of the human mind the imagination has been least explored, probably because it is the most difficult to explore... — it seems to be not only the basic and connecting link of all the finer mental powers, but in truth the knot that ties body and mind together". (cited in McFarland, 1985, p. xiii)

From Descartes' view of the imagination as at best an irrelevance and at worst an obstacle to securing knowledge, we come by the late eighteenth century to the strong role which Kant viewed it playing, in his *Critique of Pure Reason* (1781). (Though, it should be noted, in later works Kant sees a more restricted role for imagination, and in the shortened, revised version of the 1781 *Critique* [which had left his readers as bemused as Hume had left his] called the *Prologomena to Any Future Metaphysics* [1783], he does not mention it ["Einbildungskraft"] at all.) The strong role involved it in providing a synthesis of experience to the mind: this synthesis "is the mere result of the power of the imagination, a blind but indispensable function of the soul, without which we should have no knowledge whatsoever, but of which we are scarcely ever conscious. To bring this synthesis to concepts is a function which belongs to the understanding" (Kant [1781], cited in White, 1990, p. 44). What is noteworthy here is the clear distinction between the things that the imagination deals with, and concepts.

The Romantic Imagination

> The primary imagination I hold to be the living power and prime agent of all human perception and as a repetition in the finite mind of the eternal act of creation in the infinite I AM. (Coleridge, *Biographia Literaria*, Ch. XIII)

So the Romantic poet Coleridge expresses a culmination of the trends we have been following. The image of God in people is no longer seen as the soul but rather is identified in the creative imagination. Coleridge seems to be implying enthusiastically that Adam and Eve were right to eat the forbidden fruit and Prometheus was right to steal the fire, and that it is our job to exercise the creative powers we have been given.

This primary imagination echoes Kant's strong position, even if in greatly inflated language. It is that fundamental, non-voluntary, largely unconscious synthesizer of experience that is at the root of our consciousness. Coleridge distinguishes from this a "secondary imagination" which is basically similar to the primary but which works at the conscious level. It takes the material generated by our primary imagination and "dissolves, dissipates" it and uses its elements consciously to create imaginary worlds. This is the source of the artist's consciously controlled creativity; it is "essentially vital". He distinguishes further the "Fancy", which he sees as essentially mimetic, involving the combining of images from memory and the kind of ornamental but uncreative powers ascribed to imagination by most seventeenth-century and early eighteenth-century writers. (This, anyway, is how I read his distinctions, though it must be admitted that the distinctions are not altogether pellucid and one sees somewhat varied interpretations of them.)

The Romantics had inherited from the Enlightenment a conception of imagination that involved three connected functions: it was involved in perception, creating particular kinds of order and making sense of experience for us; it was a conjuror of images of what we had in the past perceived or of images made by combining elements from past perception into new forms; and it was tied into our emotions, evoking responses to what was not present as though it was present. The Romantics added, with much emphasis, that creative insight or intuition most evident in the work of the artist. This further power of imagination may be simply a result of the conscious control of the other functions working at a high pitch. But the conscious control, and the sense of the self-conscious mind as itself wonderful and worthy of exploration, provide a distinguishing characteristic to the Romantics' conception of imagination.

William Wordsworth talks of the poet as possessing

> ...a disposition to be affected more than other men by absent things as if they were present; an ability of conjuring up in himself passions which...do more nearly resemble the passions produced by real events than anything which, from the notions of their own mind merely, other men are accustomed to feel in themselves. (1802 Preface to the *Lyrical Ballads*)

This emphasizes the power of poets to respond emotionally to images they can call up at will and so, in some significant way, control their experience. But it also suggests that this poetic function of the imagination is what anyone uses, with greater or less intensity, when reflecting on the past, future, or otherwise absent.

But Wordsworth also saw the full import of Kant's "Copernican Revolution". As Copernicus had shown that the Earth orbited the Sun, and not the other way around, so Kant showed that the mind determined how the world was perceived, it did not simply produce a copy of the world delivered by the senses. So Wordsworth saw it as crucial that "Imagination...has no reference to images that are merely a faithful copy, existing in the mind, of absent external objects; but is a word of higher import, denoting operations of the mind upon these objects" (Wordsworth [1815] 1940-49, Vol. III, pp. 30-31). The *reproductive* uses of imagination — of translating perceptions into memory and up to reason, calling forth images of things once perceived, or of connecting images of things perceived with one another — which were the limits of its power that the ancient and medieval worlds recognized are not merely now transcended, they are denied. That is, the function of the imagination is such that it never merely copies the world or translates perceptions; it is a constantly active and creative faculty that shapes the world we perceive and that uses our hopes, fears, and other emotions in that shaping.

Coleridge claimed that Wordsworth's greatness was due to his combining profound thought with deep feeling. Wordsworth clearly saw this combination as another power of the imagination.

We have tended to inherit from the Romantics a sense of imagination belonging to the arts and as something distinct from the functions of our reason. But Wordsworth knew that reason and imagination were not mutually exclusive faculties, or even in any way incompatible. He declared, rather, that imagination was nothing other than "Reason in her most exalted mood" (*The Prelude*, Bk. XIV, l. 192).

The Romantics added, or gave pointed definition to, another dimension of the concept of imagination; that is, its imprecise but strong connection with childhood experience. Much of our adult intellectual activity, in this view, is stimulated by a subconscious attempt to recapture the "lost vision", the purity and power of the perception, experience and emotion of childhood. William Wordsworth is perhaps the most compelling advocate of this view. When he considers a young child playing or wandering by a stream he sees one "on whom those truths do rest / Which we are toiling all our lives to find" ("Intimations of Immortality", ll. 115/16). Consider, for a moment, the kind of food you most hated when you were five years old. Try to recapture the intensity of that loathing. Now perhaps you eat that food routinely. We often account this a triumph of character, a mark of adulthood. It is, of course, rather a result of the decay of taste-buds. Similarly, those who share Wordsworth's view claim that our experience of the world is most vivid and clear in childhood (see, e.g., Coe, 1984), and that that vividness and clarity gradually decays as we get older.

Intellectual changes with age are described almost invariably as "developments", as progress and advance. A focus on the Romantic conception of imagination suggests that this comforting story is, in part at least, a fiction. The justification for stimulation of the imagination throughout the educational process is that the imagination is the faculty which can best preserve the memory and wonder-full experience of childhood. This perception has tended to be appreciated mainly by those in whom, indeed, imagination seems most fully active: particularly poets and artists. It is an insight constantly being recovered with a kind of surprise, perhaps because it runs so starkly against the conventional view: "Perhaps true imagination, nothing to do with fantasy, consists in seeing everyday things with the eyes of our earliest days" (Paz, 1989, p. 772).

Romanticism has bequeathed to us a much enlarged conception of imagination and a new conception of the mind. During this period the classical and medieval conception of the mind as a kind of *mirror* on the world changed dramatically, such that the mind was seen as more like a *lamp*, which shines out showing a world lit by its generative energy (Abrams, 1958). In particular the Romantics were aggressive in asserting that the imaginative artist could help us to reach truth and reality no less than could the scientist: Beauty, as Keats compactly puts it, is Truth. This new conception of a creative imagination was supported by the transformation of the physical environment during the Industrial Revolution. The series of inventions, creating a new world and changes on a scale never before seen, also needed to be accounted for. While many of the Romantic poets were horrified at the industrialization of the world, this too could be recognized as a further product of the "repetition in the finite mind of the eternal act of creation". The revolutions in the political world, particularly in France, and in poetry and in people's conception of themselves, and in the material fabric of cities, factories, and railroads, led many Romantics to a high pitch of enthusiasm, and extravagant rhetoric about the imagination's powers. And while, as Kearney deflatingly observes, the "Romantic imagination could not possibly deliver on its promises" (1988, p. 185), mainly because it could only form images not realities, the monumental changes to reality in the Industrial Revolution gave people grounds to believe otherwise.

Imagination in the Modern Period: Philosophical Work

"A connection of imagination with imagery gripped the thought of so many philosophers from Aristotle to the present day so strongly that they ignored the contradiction between it and their actual use of the notion of imagination" (White, 1990, p. 6). What was true of Hume, White argues, applies equally to all other pre-twentieth-century philosophers: "Hume's own actual *use* of the concept of imagination and the words 'imagine', 'imagination' and 'imaginary' was both exactly the same as our contemporary use and yet at variance with his theory of imagination" (White, 1990, p. 42). Philosophers in this century have untied imagination from imagery, as our use of the concept of imagination requires, and have explored implications of its new freedom. (However, it should be noted that the confusion that gripped philosophers is one from which Coleridge and Wordsworth long ago broke free.)

Sartre, Wittgenstein, and Ryle have each, in quite similar ways, attacked the traditional, constricted concept of imagination articulated in previous philosophical writings. They each undermine the notion that the imagination is a faculty or distinct part of the mind whose particular functioning we might explore. Because we call some acts imaginative does not imply that there is a thing in the mind we could identify as the imagination, as the fact that we call some things fast does not imply that there is a thing in the world we could identify as speed. Similarly each of them rejects the notion that imagining something is "seeing" a mental image or quasi-picture with the "mind's eye". When imagining, however vividly, we do not see anything because there is nothing to be seen, or to see with, in the mind. When we imagine the sound of a tree falling in a deserted forest, there is no sound nor any organ in the mind for hearing it. (This is to follow Ryle's [1949] way of formulating these points.) While at one level it is obvious that seeing and hearing are different from the kind of "seeing" and "hearing" supposed to be conjured up by the imagination, it is this way of talking about our imaginative experience that has tended to lead us astray: it "is a picture created by the mentalistic vocabulary that we have inherited, and it is the pervasiveness of this vocabulary which makes it so difficult for us to avoid speaking and thinking of the imagination as a hidden faculty engaged in covert operations" (Novitz, 1987, p. 8). The difficulty is such that no-one is likely to stop talking about mental images as products of the imagination, however misleading this might have been. But, as Warnock suggests (1976, p. 196), we should not worry over-much, as such terms are increasingly recognized as metaphoric.

Of these three twentieth-century philosophers, Sartre has written most extensively about imagination. He set himself to articulate a theory of imagination that would satisfy two requirements: "It must account for the spontaneous discrimination made by the mind between its images and its perceptions; and it must explain the role that images play in the operation of thinking" (Sartre, [1940], 1972, p. 117).

Sartre set himself the task of examining with great care the phenomena of mental images. He took from the phenomenologist Husserl (1859-1938) the idea that imagination is an intentional act of consciousness rather than a thing in consciousness; it is one way in which our consciousness works, rather than a distinct part of it that might be studied separately. He concluded that one could further specify a series of characteristics of imagination. Perception and imagination, he argued, do not so much deal with different objects as represent different ways of being conscious of objects. The image of an object differs from a concept of an object in that the image provides an "intuition" of the presence of the object; concepts provide symbols of the object, without the attendant sense of presence that the imagination generates. The imaginative consciousness deals with objects *as if* they are present, while knowing clearly that they are not.

The "quasi-observation" that we experience with images is also different from perception in that it can teach us nothing we do not already know, whereas by perception we can learn new things. Sartre cites the thought experiment, in which you are asked to imagine the Parthenon. We can all bring some kind of image of it to mind. Now, count the columns. You can only do this accurately if you already know how many columns the Parthenon has. You cannot derive this knowledge from the image.

Imagination also differs from perception in that perception "receives" its objects, whereas imagination intentionally generates them. Sartre considers the imagination's capacity to intentionally make its own meanings very important. It is the condition by which "consciousness discovers its *freedom*" (Kearney, 1988, p. 227). The imagination's independence from the objective constraints of the perceived world allows it freedom over time and space. They can be stretched, reversed, obliterated or whatever. This freedom is a condition of the non-existence or the "nothingness" of the objects of imagination. Imagination then "is not an empirical and superadded power of consciousness, it is the whole of consciousness as it realizes its freedom" (Sartre, 1972, p. 270).

This is a rather Continental way of putting it, of course, but it is echoed by Sartre's English contemporary, I. A. Richards. For Richards, "*Imagination* named the active mind, the mind in action construing and constructing, dissolving and re-creating, making sense, making meaning" (Bertoff, 1990b, p. 61). Mind you, this is not all that much clearer, and sounds very like Coleridge's "secondary imagination". Both Sartre and Richards agree, however, that we will not get a clear grasp on the powers of imagination if we focus on a *part* of the mind's functioning; rather imagination is understood better as *a way in which* the mind functions when actively involved in meaning-making, in its generative mode.

Alan White criticizes Sartre, Ryle, and Wittgenstein because, when they get down to detailed analysis, they nearly always confine their attention to cases of imagining some sensory object or experience — a tree, or a friend Peter, or riding a horse, or eating a lemon. This tends to focus attention on visualizing, which in turn leads to comparisons and distinctions between imagining and seeing a particular object or experience (or remembering, hallucinating, dreaming it, etc.). If, however, one took as paradigmatic of imagination such very common cases as "I can imagine a world without war", or "I can't imagine wanting to live like that", or "I can imagine what the neighbours will think", or "I never imagined you would fail", or "Imagine her running a shoe company", or "Imagine selling your birthright for a mess of pottage", then the kind of visualization suggested by such an example as "I imagine my beloved's face" would be considered incidental. The main difficulty in dealing with the concept of imagination, as White meticulously shows, has been "a mistaken assimilation of imagination and visualization" (1990, p. 85). He reminds us that the "imagination of a theoretical thinker may be as rich or as poor, as vivid or as faint, as that of a painter" (1990, p. 89), and that we have imaginary troubles as often as we hear imaginary noises. So "imagining and forming an image are not the same" (1990, p. 90).

And, reciprocally, we can have images, in dreams or aroused by conversation, without our imagining anything. One can distinguish between visualizing and imagining by reflecting on the fact that to visualize Jane would be the same as to visualize her identical twin sister, Giaconda, but to imagine Jane would be distinct from imagining Giaconda; or you could imagine a suitcase completely obscuring a cat but not visualize it in a way distinct from simply visualizing a suitcase. (I have taken most of the examples in this paragraph from White.)

Even in literature, which is the area of human thought and expression where the evoking of sensuous, quasi-pictorial images is often considered most active, one has to agree that "much great literature does not evoke sensuous images, or, if it does, it does so only incidentally, occasionally and intermittently. In the depiction even of a fictional character the writer may not suggest visual images at all....If we had to visualize every metaphor in poetry we would become completely bewildered and confused" (Wellek and Warren, 1949, pp. 26/27).

White concludes that to "imagine something is to *think of* it as possibly being so" (1990, p. 184), and that an "imaginative person is one with the ability to think of lots of possibilities, usually with some richness of detail" (1990, p. 185), and that the "very imaginative child not only thinks of and treats the chair as a fortress, but fills it, in word and deed, with a wealth of possible detail" (1990, p. 186). He adds that imagination "is linked to discovery, invention and originality because it is thought of the possible rather than the actual" (1990, p. 186). This seems close to Sartre's notion of imagination as what empowers us to conceive of possibilities in or beyond the actualities in which we are immersed, and as such the key to our sense of freedom. It also calls up Brian Sutton-Smith's throwaway suggestion that imagination is the subjunctive mood of mind (1988, p. 19). It also recalls Paul Ricoeur's notion that imagination involves us not just in seeing actualities, but "suddenly we are 'seeing as'.... we see old age as the close of day, time as a beggar, nature as a temple with living pillars, and so forth" (1978, p. 8). If the mood of imagination is the subjunctive, its trope is metaphor.

"Being able to think of the possible" may seem something of a letdown after our pursuit of imagination as intermediary between sense and mind, and as implicated in our sensations themselves, or as connected with "lively passions", or as our share in the creative power of God. When we commend people for varied forms of imaginativeness, are we always commending their capacity to think about possibilities? Implied in White's discussion is the sense of the possibilities being useful, appropriate, or fulfilling. This leads us to Barrow's neat formulation: to be imaginative is "to have the tendency and ability consciously to conceive the unusual and effective in a variety of particular contexts" (Barrow, 1990, p. 107). This blends well with Steen Halling's observation with regard to interpersonal relations: "We speak of a person as being imaginative insofar as he or she responds to an interpersonal crisis or impasse in a way that is unexpected and yet nonetheless appropriate and fruitful with respect to accomplishing a favourable outcome or resolution" (1987, p. 140). So if imagination, following White, is the capacity to think of possibilities, and the commendatory sense of being imaginative, following Barrow, involves thinking of unusual and effective possibilities, are we finally home and dry?

One thing, at least, seems to have been left behind in these formulations; they do not imply its absence so much as ignore it. The missing element is one considered crucial by Mary Warnock. She gathers the ideas of Hume and Kant about the imagination's role in perception and blends them with the generative or productive sense worked out in Romanticism. From the mix emerges her conclusion:

> There is a power in the human mind which is at work in our everyday perception of the world, and is also at work in our thoughts about what is absent; which enables us to see the world, whether present or absent as significant....And this power, though it gives us 'thought-imbued' perception...is not only intellectual. Its impetus comes from the emotions as much as from the reason. (1976, p. 196)

Warnock, following Sartre, argues, as have many before her, that there is an irreducible affective component in any use of imagination. Certainly if we revisit some of the examples used above, we may be inclined to agree with her. In cases like "I can't imagine living like that", or "Imagine her running a shoe company", or "Imagine selling your birthright for a mess of pottage", one might readily admit that they both express and evoke not a set of quasi-pictures in the mind but rather emotions. They are thoughts about possibilities, but they also carry feelings about the possibilities. The question is whether this affective component is a necessary element in imagining or a desirable element for making imagining more powerful, varied, appropriate, unusual and effective or an element necessary for certain kinds of imagining but not others.

This is another of those questions I will not answer here, and could not answer anywhere — to borrow G. K. Chesterton's delightful cop-out. We can observe straightforwardly, I think, that a considerable range of imaginative activity is distinctly affect-laden. Imagining is most commonly not a kind of thinking from which our feelings are excluded. Yet we can sensibly talk about a mathematician performing an imaginative calculation, which seems on the face of it not to require any affective component in the thinking itself, even if a sense of triumph or delight might infuse the achievement. Though perhaps the exploration of possible directions — the probing in various directions for a solution that fits, that is appropriate, that is "pretty", or that is aesthetically satisfying — cannot be performed without some affective engagement. And perhaps it is precisely this affective engagement — this probing of possibilities for that which fits — which distinguishes the imaginative from the conventional mathematician. Certainly mathematicians' accounts of their major breakthroughs support both a significant affective component and also a common recourse to quasi-pictorial images (Shepard, 1988). When our imaginations are evoked or stimulated by something, it seems rare that there is not also an affective tug that comes with it; as John Stuart Mill put it: "The imaginative emotion which an idea, when vividly conceived, excites in us is not an illusion but a fact, as real as any other qualities of objects" (cited in Warnock, 1976, p. 206). Still, we might wisely leave the question of whether there is a necessary affective component in any imaginative act open.

This sense of the imagination as our capacity to think of possibilities is congruent with Ricoeur's characterization of its role in our mental life as performing a "prospective and explorative function" (1965, p. 126). It is by means of imagination — to use the language of phenomenologists — that we make ourselves, seeing the directions in which we might move and the possible selves we might inhabit. It leads to formulations such as Elya Prigogine's "The real is the realization of one of many possibilities" (cited in Halling, 1987, p. 140).

Imagination in the Modern Period: Psychological Work

Philosophers' conclusion that imagination is a kind of thinking that commonly does not involve forming images in the mind or dealing at all with examining quasi-pictures in "the mind's eye", must initially leave us a little uncertain of what to make of contemporary psychological work, which has taken such assumed phenomena as its subject matter. Let us consider this psychological work briefly, and see what implications we might infer from it about imagination.

With the development of experimental psychology in the late nineteenth century we see a different kind of attempt to come to grips with imagination. Sir Francis Galton conducted research — initially a questionnaire — to "elicit the degree in which different persons possess the power of seeing images in their mind's eye, and of reviving past sensations" (Galton, 1883, p. 255). He discovered, much to his surprise, that a number of his colleagues claimed that they did not form images at all, but that most women, children and "people of the labouring class" claimed to be able to "visualize" vividly images of past conditions, such as the contents, and colours, of their breakfast tables (Galton, 1883). As refined abstract thinking was most highly valued in the sciences, visualizing and image-forming seem to have become generally considered a more "primitive" form of thought — to use Galton's term. After all, if women, children, and labourers could manage it easily and vividly and his intellectual colleagues often did not manage it at all, it was clearly a skill to be associated with lower-level intellectual functioning.

This disrepute tended to persist within science, and perhaps even more so within a psychology that has been eager to be considered scientific. John B. Watson, "the father of behaviourism", considered attempts to study imagination and mental images pointless, as they entailed no measurable behaviours. Howard Gardner describes the subsequent history of the imagination in psychological research:

> There was no reliable way to define imagery in an experimental situation, no agreement about what should count as an imagistic or imaginary experience....For such reasons, the ghostly image was exorcised for half a century from respectable academic psychology. (1985, p. 324)

In some psychological circles this disrepute and neglect continue. But through this century the most successful physicists and mathematicians, when asked to account for their discoveries or most famous breakthroughs, have very frequently described images as crucial (Shepard, 1988). Perhaps the best known is Einstein's description of imagining himself riding on a light-beam as leading to the theories of relativity. In the wake of such accounts, it has become fashionable to admit to experiencing vivid mental imagery, and mental images have again become a subject for serious psychological research (Kosslyn, 1983).

Given the research methods available to psychologists, their focus has largely been determined by whatever features of imagination seem to induce some behavioural correlate. This has led in particular to a focus on images. Perhaps because this precisely focussed research clearly deals with something much more restricted than what people usually refer to by "imagination", that term has almost entirely been replaced in the psychology literature by terms such as "imagery", "imaged", "imaging", and so on.

Recent work has been stimulated by findings such as Allan Paivio's that word pairs which were readily "imagable" were more memorable than those which could not be so readily "imaged"

(Paivio, 1965). He thereby showed that it was indeed possible to demonstrate in experimental situations effects of the kinds of mental phenomena behaviourists had exorcised (Paivio, 1971). Important work was also done on how people respond physically to their images; for example, on how people's closed eyes typically "scan" images of recently seen maps or geometrical shapes. Shepard and Metzler's (1971) work was largely responsible for launching this particular branch of research, and it has been significantly developed by Kosslyn and his associates (1980). Gardner claims that this research has "delineated major properties of the imagery system" (1985, p. 326).

After having been so neglected for so long, the study of mental imagery has become what Block describes as "one of the hottest topics in cognitive science" (1981, p. 1). But the way the topic is pursued in cognitive science seems somewhat at odds with philosophical work on imagination. In the psychological literature, mental imagery is usually defined something like "some representation of the perceptual experiences stored in a manner that the pattern recognition mechanisms can make use of them" (Lindsay and Norman, 1977, p. 414). This is a definition that, shorn of its modern technical language, seems very close to Aristotle's and Hume's. In cognitive psychology, imaging seems to exist only as a substructure of memory, in that it occurs in the process of trying to remember something. ("Memory refers to that part of the soul to which imagination refers," Aristotle, *De Memoria*, 450a.) Cognitive science research certainly seems to return us to conceptions of images as representations manipulable or "scannable" in the mind. The response of philosophers tends to be dismissive: "The discovery by psychologists that we can 'manipulate our images' no more shows that the images are entities than a discovery that we could make pains or itches move up and down our leg would show that these were entities" (White, 1990, p. 124). This observation might in turn be dismissed by psychologists as irrelevant to their model-building procedures. Harder to dismiss, perhaps, are the severe criticisms of psychologists such as Pylyshyn (1979, 1984), who make not unrelated points: e.g., developing a point by Hebb that "what people report is properties not of their image but of the objects that they are imaging" (Pylyshyn, 1981, p. 153).

Imagery, as it is usually dealt with in cognitive science, is assumed to have some sensory content (e.g., scannable images) because it is assumed to be a revived sensation. It is this conception of images that we have seen discredited in the philosophical literature, and that poses a problem for the relationship between cognitive science research on imagery and the study of imagination. But, as Murray notes, "[m]ental imagery, of course, is not to be identified with imagination, but neither is it to be dismissed as totally unrelated" (1987, p. 176). So, while current psychological research on imagery seems better characterized as related to memory of previous perceptions than to imagination, it would be incautious therefore to dismiss its findings as of no relevance, and imprudent to ignore the potential value for education of findings such as Paivio's.

Conclusion

"To imagine something is to *think of* it as possibly being so" (White, 1990, p. 184). This terse formulation sums up a considerable range of attempts to grasp the complex nature of imagination. It captures both the sense in which we can conceive of the world as other than it is, with flying horses and ourselves ruling it, and also the sense in which the historian or physicist or any of us strives to conceive of the world exactly as it is. The former encompasses one of the commonest senses evident in our very short history, the latter encompasses Coleridge's sense of imagination as thinking that is unsubdued by habit, unshackled by custom, and as that which enables us to transcend those obstacles to seeing the world as it is that are placed before us by conventional, inadequate interpretations and representations. Both senses of this capacity to think of something as possibly being so, point to the imagination as the source of novelty, originality, and generativity.

When we commend someone as imaginative we imply that they have this capacity in a high degree. Imaginativeness is not a well-developed, distinct function of the mind, but is rather a particular flexibility which can invigorate all mental functions. We recognize the imaginative person by the impact in some particular realm of their unusual and effective thinking — to use Barrow's joint criteria. So, in language use imaginativeness may be evident in speech by wit, in thought by insight, in planning by ingenuity, and so on. The flexibility that is central to imaginativeness seems to enable the imaginative person to conceive of a wider than normal range of states or actions that do not exist or that do not follow by literal extrapolation from current states or actions or from conventional representations of states or actions. In conceiving an indeterminate range of such states or actions the imaginative person can hold them in the mind, consider potential implications, assess their appropriateness, or scan their features, selecting whichever might be most unusual and effective. (People who produce effective but conventional plans, language, ideas or whatever, we would consider sensible or sound but not imaginative.) In pursuing this sense of imagination in action, I realize that I have approached a model not unlike that articulated by Arthur Koestler in his *The Act of Creation* (1964). This suggests that creativity might be considered as the outward expression of imagination working in a high degree.

Unfortunately the way I have characterized imaginativeness above suggests a sequence in which the imaginative person first generates and then evaluates the range of possibilities. If instead we accept Sharon Bailin's characterization (1988) in which evaluation goes on in the act of generation, we would not preclude forms of thinking that are clearly unusual and effective but that seem to move directly to the most fruitful possibility. That is, the above characterization is not an attempt to provide a literal description of a *process* of thinking. Rather it should be taken as an attempt to capture features of imaginativeness in a graspable form; so "flexibility", for example, should not be read literally as a power of generating endless possibilities interrupted by a selecting mechanism. As long as we recognize that "flexibility" and "scanning" and "selecting", and so on, are significantly metaphoric we need not be led to inappropriate simplification.

There is a sense of "imagination" that has recurred prominently in the very short history above which does not fit with White's formulation. David Hume was the most articulate advocate, and Mary Warnock a modern proponent, of implicating imagination in creating coherence and meaning at the basic level of perception. I want to touch on this, not to try to incorporate this sense into our conception of imagination, but to exclude it. The origins of seeing imagination as implicated in the most basic level of making perceptual sense of the world we found in the belief that all the contents of the mind had their origin in prior perception. The senses were the only source from which ideas could have come, and the ability to recall images of things seen in the past served as a paradigm of how imagination somehow could invade the memory and represent salient features of remembered perceptions, but also combine and transform them at will. Given that Hume believed sense impressions were the only source of all our knowledge and concepts, the somewhat magical faculty of imagination became his chosen candidate for transmuting impressions into ideas. One cannot but feel, at this remove, that there was something a little arbitrary in Hume's deployment of imagination for this role. Warnock's recent championing of something like Hume's view is a little harder to understand. She claims that imagination "is involved in all perception of the world, in that it is that element in perception which makes what we see and hear meaningful to us" (Warnock, 1977, p. 152). Now Warnock's claim is different from Hume's in that her point is that imagination is what heightens our perceptions and allots significance and meaning to them. In particular she is interested in the role of emotion and value in doing so. But, at least in the form she has developed this sense of imagination, and more obviously in the way Hume deployed it, it seems to conflict with two features of the conception being developed here.

It conflicts first with the sense of imagining as a conscious, intentional activity. Daydreaming, for example, slides over into imaginative activity only when we assume the director's seat; a dream can slide into imaginative activity only when we wake and recognize its unreality. Imagination, as Sartre and Wittgenstein both emphasized, works consciously knowing the unreality of its objects. Imagination operating "in all perception of the world" does not require conscious or intentional intervention and, at least in Hume's sense, is a capacity we share with cats, dogs, and earthworms. The second conflict concerns the arbitrariness of Hume's deployment of "imagination" to plug a gap in his account of how knowledge is generated and grows in the mind. Very few people today believe that such an account is anything like correct, despite its historical importance for psychology and philosophy. Given that modern accounts do not look for some faculty to transmute world stuff into mind stuff, that role for, and conception of, imagination is obsolete. So, we will probably have a more coherent and adequate grasp on imagination if we jettison the notion that it is implicated in all our perception of the world.

White's formulation lacks any references to images. His work, and much of the philosophical research of this century, has been concerned to show that imaginative thinking does not require images, and that those accounts of the imagination that conceived it as primarily the capacity to form images were either wrong or relevant only to some kinds of imaginative thinking. White summarizes this point: "The presence or absence of imagery depends only on what kind of thing is imagined in either of these ways; is it perceptual or non-perceptual" (1990, p. 188). But the presence or absence of images does not seem to be a simple binary condition; rather it has been clear from common experience and from Galton's research, and much other research since, that there is a continuum from vivid quasi-pictorial images, through more partial images, to the most fleeting, impressionistic evocations that may feel more like moods or emotions but which nevertheless have some imagistic component.

Again White emphasizes that a "vivid imagination is not the ability to 'see' or 'hear' things clearly in our mind, nor, as philosophers from Descartes to Hume thought, merely to rearrange 'ideas', that is material previously received through the senses, but to think of varied, detailed and, perhaps, unusual and hitherto unthought possibilities, whether or not these include perceptual and, therefore, imageable features. The imagination of a genius is not necessarily linked to his faculty of forming images" (1990, p. 192). If by "image" we mean vivid quasi-pictures or quasi-sounds, then this seems likely the case. But if "image" refers to something towards the other end of the continuum suggested above, then matters are rather less clear. Imagining Medieval Christendom, or what the neighbours will think, or selling one's birthright for a mess of pottage certainly *can* involve fleeting, partial, insubstantial images. And while Shepard's (1988) research does not establish a necessary link between the imagination of a genius and his or her faculty of forming images, it does show that this link is much more common even in non-perceptual topics in mathematics and theoretical physics than had commonly been thought to be the case.

The evoking of images, as Sartre argues with a range of examples, seems to have an irreducible affective component. And if we resist that "irreducible", we have to acknowledge that an affective component is common. That is, the imagination enables us to feel about something not present or even real as though it were real and present. The commonly observed link between imagination and emotions, especially in cases where images are consciously evoked, is one of some relevance here; as is the common observation that when we sustain a sequence of images in the mind they move in a narrative, riding on metaphoric connections. So that nexus of affect, narrative, and metaphor is commonly brought into play when we exercise the image-forming capacities of imagination. The discovery of oral cultures concerning the power of images for holding information or ideas in the mind, has tended to be depreciated during the period of "high literacy", in which the abstract concept has played a more valued role in intellectual life than the affective image.

My point in raising this complicated, if fashionable, set of topics — image, emotion, narrative, metaphor — is due to my desire to leave open a question White's formulation seems to close down. His work has marginalized the image in conceiving of imagination, arguing that the presence or absence of images turns only on whether one is imagining something with or without perceptual qualities. I think it should remain open as to whether evoking (sometimes fleeting, partial, barely acknowledged) images is part of all uses of the imagination. Imagining selling one's birthright for a mess of pottage or what the neighbours will think or Medieval Christendom may indeed not necessarily call up detailed quasi-pictures as does imagining the face of one's beloved. But imagining selling one's birthright for a mess of pottage, at least for me, crowds behind the concept an indeterminate mass of images, half-images, fleeting Old Testament scenes, perhaps pictured in childhood, particular parents and children, bowls of pottage, and so on; Medieval Christendom has, thronging behind and sustaining the concept, images of Popes, pilgrims, half-remembered pictures of St. Francis and St. Dominic, monasteries in modern ruins or ancient operation, and so on; "what the neighbours will think" is supported by images of particular neighbours, some long dead, incidents in which their thinking was significant, of garden walls and fences, houses, and so on. The imagined concept can be dealt with abstractly, but once imagined it seems to serve as an identifier, evoker, and retriever of a range of images that, as it were, line up or throng up behind it ready for easy access to conscious contemplation. The images seem not necessarily evoked or retrieved by any logical classificatory system but rather by emotional, or metaphoric, or even sonorous associations. So the mess of pottage brings into bizarre, but typical, association Jacob and Esau, Scottish crofters eating porridge, prodigal sons, school-day breakfasts, clam chowder, and on and on. This realm of associated images underlying concepts is one that Freud explored to interesting effect. My point here is that if imagination entails, even in some vestigial forms, this kind of evoking of images even when we deal with abstract ideas, then the point Warnock emphasizes about the necessary affective component in imagination applies not only to those obvious cases of vivid and dramatic quasi-pictorial images but to all uses of imagination. That is, it lets the wild animals that come along with images into the domesticated concept from which White excludes them. This is an issue that will not be decided by individual witness to what seems to be the case when one imagines things, but such cases might suggest, at least, that we not conclude unqualifiedly that the role of images in imagination is unimportant in forming an adequate grasp on it.

More straightforwardly, however, we find the emotions aroused with the imagination because what drives us to think of things as possibly being so is commonly tied to our hopes, fears, and intentions.

I would like to make one final observation, more in harmony with White's formulation. This concerns the relationship of imagination and rationality. Wordsworth's claim that imagination denotes amplitude of mind and reason in her most exalted mood catches two topics of relevance here. "Amplitude of mind" reflects the observation already made about imaginativeness entailing flexibility, variability, richness of detail, unusualness in thinking. That imagination should also and relatedly be considered "Reason in her most exalted mood" may seem rather less obvious. The common distinction between reason and imagination made through much of the very short history above is one that remains influential still. There is certainly a tendency in educational writings to see them as more or less discrete, and mutually antipathetic, categories, even to the extent that some areas of the curriculum are largely assumed to address and develop one and other areas are largely assumed to address and develop the other — science and mathematics are commonly taken to deal mainly with reason and the arts with imagination. (There is an element of simplification if not caricature here, but much less than one might wish.)

Identifying imagination in the capacity to think of something as possibly being so, certainly does not suggest any conflict with rationality. Rather, the ability to hold alternative conceptions in the mind and assess their adequacy or appropriateness would seem a necessary component of any sophisticated rational activity. "How, Solomon, can you rationally decide between the competing claims of two women each claiming custody of a child on the grounds of being the mother?" The rational resolution was neither a matter of literal calculation nor formal logic, and neither would one suggest that Solomon behaved irrationally. Rather, it was a case of reason in her most exalted mood.

We might consider David Hammond's (1990) adaption of Gerard Manley Hopkins' term and conceive of imagination as the "inscape" of rationality. This certainly obliterates the false and destructive dichotomizing of the two and suggests an enriched and expanded sense of rationality. With imagination as its "inscape", we can see how the capacity to conceive of possible worlds enables us rationally to probe alternatives and to explore beyond what is conventionally represented or can be formally or literally extrapolated from what is or seems to be the case. The slight difficulty with this is that it tends to suggest both that all rational thinking must involve some degree of imaginativeness and that irrationality lacks imaginativeness. Neither of these suggestions seem warranted (nor does Hammond's use imply that they are).

So, imagination is the capacity to think of things as possibly being so; it is an intentional act of mind; it is the source of invention, novelty, and generativity; it is not implicated in all perception and in the construction of all meaning; it is not distinct from rationality but is rather a capacity that greatly enriches rational thinking. The imaginative person has this capacity in a high degree. It may not be invariably true that imagination involves our image-forming capacity, but image-forming is certainly common in uses of the imagination and *may* in subtle ways be inevitably involved in all forms of imagining; and image-forming commonly implicates emotions.

CHAPTER TWO

Why Is Imagination Important to Education?

Introduction

Given the concept of imagination that our very short history has led us towards, let us now turn to education and see why the development of this kind of imagination should be considered important. While everyone seems to be generally in favour of imagination, it is worth trying to spell out in some detail reasons why its development is educationally important. First, spelling out such reasons can help us design practices and environments that will more likely stimulate students' imaginations. Second, spelling them out can uncover perhaps unexpected educational implications of our concept of imagination. Third, prevailing conceptions of imagination are very varied and, on the whole, vague, and they are also biased towards suggesting that imagination and reason are somehow discrete intellectual activities, so spelling out reasons why the concept articulated in the previous chapter is important to education may counter the influence of more restricted conceptions. Fourth, the prevailing rather diffuse support for developing imagination in education is largely restricted to the arts, with an anaemic support for novelty in some other curriculum areas, so spelling out reasons why the above concept is important to education should help to extend the sense of imagination's proper role in all areas of the curriculum. And, fifth, it must be said that the typical structures and practices of current schooling, as detailed in a wealth of reports, are designed according to principles and priorities which clearly do not consider any sense of imagination very important to education — at least, the word very rarely appears in such reports; spelling out reasons why the above concept is important to education might encourage even those with the most utilitarian view of the role of schools to take imagination more seriously.

Many educationalists have addressed various of the topics I will raise below, and there is a rich and valuable literature about imagination in education. It is, however, much smaller in scale than the amount of writing and research on logico-mathematical forms of thinking, and also it is difficult to find any significant body of educational research that addresses imaginative thinking. But while this literature and some research exists, I do not intend this chapter to be in any sense a review of it. This is not at all intended to depreciate the literature and research which addresses imagination, but is due simply to my relatively narrow aim of carrying forward the conception of imagination developed above into education. So much of the current literature assumes, and uses, more vague and general concepts that building from that literature explicitly — rather than implicitly, as I certainly do — would involve a kind of philosophical qualification of meanings such that the simpler purpose of the chapter might get buried. So I will try to point briefly to a range of reasons why imagination is important to education, well aware that I will be frequently covering well-trodden ground. My aim is hardly originality, but just an extension of the previous discussion into educational issues.

Imagination and Conventional Thinking

When we look at typical educational practice, we would be justified in assuming that the main purpose of education is to ensure that students accumulate knowledge, skills, and attitudes appropriate for the lives they are likely to lead. But when we look at the writings of the greatest educational thinkers we find that their main concern is rather different from this. If we consider Plato, Rousseau, and Dewey, for example, it is clear that the accumulation of knowledge and skills in the sense that seems to exercise our schools almost exclusively, is only a small part of what concerns them. What seems to be central to becoming educated in their view is not being bound by the conventional ideas and beliefs which people commonly grow up to accept. Education, they passionately assert, is about something that we typically attend to very little in our schools. Instilling knowledge is obviously not irrelevant to them, but their concerns with it are determined by the much more important question of how one enables a student to become an autonomous thinker, able to see conventional ideas for what they are. Education, to put it a bit tendentiously, is a process that awakens individuals to a kind of thought that enables them to imagine conditions other than those that exist or that have existed.

This way of putting it may seem tendentious because it suggests that imagination, in the sense articulated above, is central to what the greatest educational theorists were concerned to stimulate. Certainly the programmes that these great educationalists proposed in order to carry young children to educated adulthood differ radically, one from the other. Plato proposed a tightly regimented curriculum taking fifty years to ensure freeing his best students' minds from the constrictions of *doxa* or conventional opinion. Rousseau proposed manipulating his student's every thought and preventing him from learning to read until about twelve years old, so that he would not be infected by all the second-hand ideas of ordinary social discourse and of books. Dewey proposed methods of instruction designed to encourage students to adopt a scientific, inquiring and skeptical attitude.

It does not seem inappropriate to identify as common to these programmes a concern to stimulate in students the ability to think of things as possibly being so, with all that implies in terms of flexibility, richness, and freedom of mental activity. The failure of education, for these educational thinkers, is evident not so much in ignorance as in imprisonment of the mind by conventional ideas. Imagination entails the ability to transcend the obstacles to thinking with which easy acceptance of conventional beliefs, ideas, interpretations, representations, and so on, confront us.

Conventional minds may be encyclopaedically well-informed and perform superbly on scholastic achievement tests and have stratospherically elevated I.Q.s, and so on. A. N. Whitehead has referred to such people as the greatest bores on God's earth. Such intellectual skills, when not enlivened by imagination, lack the ingredient that makes them educationally alive. We all recognize the inappropriateness of calling "educated" either a dull pedant who may be enormously well-informed about some area of knowledge or a quiz-show whiz with a superb memory for show-biz trivia. That is, knowing a lot, or even being "culturally literate" in E. D. Hirsch, Jr.'s sense (1987), implies nothing about being able to think in ways that can transcend conventional ideas. Imagination is what enables this transcendence, and is consequently necessary to education. It is important because transcending the conventional is necessary to constructing one's sense of any area of knowledge; accepting conventional representations is to fail to make knowledge one's own, is to keep it inert rather than incorporate it into one's life.

There is, of course, a constant tension in education between teaching the conventions whereby students will have to live and encouraging the capacities that enable them to gain some kind of mental freedom from those conventions — making them tools rather than constraints. This tension is prominent in the writings of the great educational thinkers, but unfortunately rather less prominent in many schools. The former part of the job, the socializing or inducting students into current conventions, seems to predominate. And this observation is not intended to underestimate how difficult it is to do even this job properly. The power to be free of conventions tends to be cultivated much less, for many reasons: it is hard; we have no clear curriculum guidelines for achieving it; it clashes with what already takes up so much energy; and of course the school's bureaucratic needs for order and various kinds of regimentation exert subtle but powerful pressures against it. But if we are to take education seriously we must take development of the imagination seriously, and this will rarely sit comfortably with settled conventions.

This also represents a challenge to the teacher, of course. Given our graded schools, with maybe thirty children in each class, conventional thinking that conforms with the expectations built into worksheets and textbooks and other activities to be performed in common is very readily accepted and rewarded by teachers as most appropriate and valued. This is not to say that imagination is necessarily at odds with successfully achieving routine tasks. Rather it is to emphasize that the structures of our educational institutions can tend to encourage precisely the forms of efficient conventional thinking that the greatest educational thinkers have identified as one of the enemies of education. The challenge for the teacher is constantly to ensure that worksheet, textbook, and other activities allow or lead into thinking about the possible as well as the actual. How we might go about this is the subject of later chapters.

Imagination in Learning

Since the invention of writing, we have developed elaborate means of storing information. One feature of these systems of storage and recall, whether on wax-tablets, parchment, in books, or in computers is that what you put in is what you get out. Human learning is in significant ways different from such storage and retrieval. But unfortunately our technologies influence the ways we think about ourselves. Certainly if you think about learning a fact — say, that water boils at 100 degrees Celsius at sea level — and then repeating that fact later, what you have done looks very like what happens if the fact is recorded somewhere in symbols and then later retrieved. It just so happens that in this case the storage device is your brain and the retrieval mechanism is your memory.

If we allow our technologies to determine how we think about our intellectual processes, then one effect, which has been pervasive and very damaging to education, is to think of learning as a process analogous to recording symbols in the mind for later retrieval. The first thing we might note is that the human mind seems to be really quite inefficient at this kind of recording and faithful preservation over time. A sheet of paper or a computer disk is much more reliable. Learning in this technology-analogous sense can be measured by how faithfully the records have been preserved when retrieved on a later test. This kind of testing goes on all the time in schools, and the results are taken very straightforwardly as evidence of learning. This has been going on so long and so ubiquitously in schools that the meaning of learning that is most common is this kind of mechanical storage and retrieval.

And what's wrong with that? Well, a number of things. Most generally what's wrong is that it ignores what is distinctive about human learning. In particular it leads to people forgetting that the human mind learns quite unlike the way a computer "learns", and that our memories are quite unlike computer "memories".

The human mind does not simply store facts discretely when it learns. Perhaps it *can* do this, and we might occasionally use this capacity to remember a phone number or a shopping list in the absence of a piece of paper. More typically when we learn even the simplest fact — that Vasco da Gama set off from Lisbon to sail around Africa in 1497 or that spiders have eight legs — we do not simply lodge these as discrete data in our brains. When learned, they mix in with the complex of shifting emotions, memories, intentions, and so on that constitute our mental lives. Facts about spiders will gain an affective colouring connected with our feelings about insects in general and about spiders in particular. Vasco da Gama's voyages may trigger images of ships off alien coasts and a sense of adventure. Whether and *how* we learn and retain these particular facts is affected by the complex of meaning-structures we already have in place, which in turn are affected by our emotions, intentions, and so on.

The human memory is not an orderly place with slots or shelves for each item to remain inertly until called for. It is more like a shifting turmoil stirred by those emotions and intentions that are a part of us. Virtually nothing emerges from the human memory in the same form it was initially learned. All kinds of associations curl around each new fact, there is endless blending and coalescing, and connections are made, broken, and remade. And no small part of this activity involves the imagination. The more energetic and lively the imagination, the more are facts constantly finding themselves in new combinations and taking on new emotional colouring as we use them to think of possibilities, of possible worlds.

It is becoming clear that human learning does not involve simply mirroring what is outside the mind, but crucially involves *constructing* or *composing* (Bruner, 1986). Each mind is different and is a different perspective on the world. In the process of learning, the student has to fit whatever is to be learned into his or her unique complex of meaning-structures that are already in place. This requires restructuring, composition, and reassessment of meanings. And it is in this ascribing of meaning that Warnock identifies one of the fundamental activities of imagination. The more flexibly we can think of things as possibly being so, the richer, and the more unusual and effective can be the meanings we compose.

A separate argument is hardly required to show why the ability to learn in a way that entails the composition or construction of richer meaning is of educational importance. Taking imagination seriously, however, will require us to give up on some features of the currently dominant concept of "learning". That might seem easy enough. The difficult part, though, may be to take seriously the implications of such a decision. And this is where taking imagination seriously begins to play havoc with some of the familiar, established elements of the current educational scene. All those procedures of teaching, testing and curriculum that see education as a process of accumulating knowledge and skills uninvolved with emotions, intentions, and human meaning, will tend to be inadequate to do more than create conventional thinkers.

A common observation about imaginatively engaged learning is that it gives pleasure. Commenius long ago argued that if we arranged learning properly children would come to school with as much joy as they go to the fair. It might be optimistic to expect this routinely, but we surely all recognize times of imaginative learning that have given intense pleasure. We might usefully focus research on distinguishing the characteristics of such learning, as clarifying these would surely offer a great benefit to education. I am suggesting that we will likely find clues if we focus attention on imagination.

For the teacher this means that conventional tests of learning give what philosophers call necessary but not sufficient evidence. The classroom, to conform with the requirements of imaginative learning, has to be more hospitable to students' emotions. Genuine education inescapably involves emotional engagement. This does not mean tears, anguish and shouts of joy all day long, but it does mean that we will want to consider qualities of students' experience as part of our evidence of imaginative learning. When we hear ourselves saying "You've just got to learn it", requiring that students work at tasks even when they are unable to see the point, then we should be alerted to the fact that such learning has lost hold on students' imaginations. We cannot reasonably expect students to be pleasurably engaged all the time, and hard work is necessary for any worthwhile educational achievement, but if we accept that imaginative engagement is a necessary condition of educationally valuable learning then we will want to find ways of ensuring a place for emotion, for engaging with students' hopes, fears and intentions, and for evaluating qualities of experience and richness of meaning.

Imagination and Memory

We have seen in the previous chapter the long connection between memory and imagination. This connection is not merely an historical curiosity but remains crucially important for education today. There is a tendency that has grown out of the rhetoric of progressivism to consider that "rote-learning", or learning in the conventional sense discussed above, is educationally useless. The valuable insight in this, about the pointlessness of treating students like storage devices for knowledge that is meaningless to them, has tended occasionally to be uncritically generalized to a hostility to any kind of memorization. One of the clear implications of the consistent observation of the relationship between memory and imagination is the importance of memorizing knowledge, facts, chunks of prose and poetry, formulae, etc. for the stimulation and development of the imagination. Ignorance, in short, starves the imagination. And we are ignorant of all that knowledge which we might know how to access, but haven't, or which we have learned how to learn, but haven't. Only knowledge in our memories is accessible to the action of the imagination. We can only construct possible worlds, can only think of things as possibly being so, out of what we already know. The imagination is limited to working with what exists in the memory. As Sartre's thought experiment shows, we cannot get information from imaginative activity. But the richness, variedness, unusualness, and effectiveness of our imaginative activity will turn in significant degree on how much it has to compose or construct with.

This principle might seem to run into conflict with that of the previous section. There I seem to be arguing that the imagination is suppressed if students are set to learn lots of knowledge and skills and here I am claiming that the imagination requires the memorization of lots of knowledge and skills to be adequately stimulated. The two principles are consistent when we observe the point made above about the meaningfulness of the knowledge and skills that are to be memorized; ensuring that knowledge and skills are meaningful requires engaging the imagination in the process of learning. *How* we can go about ensuring this kind of imaginative learning is the theme of the remaining chapters of this book. What it is important to establish here, however, is that the development of students' imaginations will not go forward without their learning and memorizing much and diverse knowledge.

This has been a constant theme in what have been called "neo-conservative" educational writings during the late 1980s (e.g., Bloom, 1987; Hirsch, 1987; Ravitch & Finn, 1987). The emphasis in these neo-conservative writings has been to make the valuable point that education is crucially tied up with knowledge, and that being educated means, put crudely, knowing a lot. But, as I stressed above, it means not only that. Education is also crucially about the *meaning* knowledge has for the individual, and that is where the imagination is vital. A person who has meticulously followed the neo-conservative kind of curriculum may still end up among the greatest bores on God's earth. What is absent from those books is attention to, and a clear sense of, how knowledge becomes meaningful in the lives of learners; how we can ensure that students engage, in the sense I am developing the phrase here, in *imaginative learning*.

The average classroom is not the ideal place for this kind of memorization perhaps. But this principle suggests that teachers should give more homework or library assignments that involve memorization than is currently common. Such memorizing is often hard work; it is easier to go through another worksheet, answer a multiple-choice test on a reading, or write up a report. Keeping clearly in mind how the human memory is unlike a book or a computer may help us to recognize that memorized knowledge is one of the necessary foods of the imagination, and so may encourage us to ensure that our students simply learn a lot. Taken by itself, of course, such a recommendation could lead to much mind-numbing activity, but taken in the context of the other principles here, it seems an important and recently somewhat neglected constituent of the education of the imagination.

Social Virtues

I want to add to the list of educational values that follow from the development of the imagination such social virtues as tolerance and justice. Of course it would be too much to say that the evils of the world are due simply to a lack of imagination, but some of them seem to be so. The lack of that capacity of the imagination which enables us to understand that other people are unique, distinct, and autonomous — with lives and hopes and fears quite as real and important as our own — is evident in much evil. To understand and feel this adequately requires thinking that transcends our conventional sense of the "other". The development of that imaginative insight does not, however, guarantee that we will then treat others as we wish to be treated ourselves, but it is a necessary prerequisite. Even imagining the possible consequences of our behaviour might enhance our social virtuousness.

But there are more particular connections to be made between the imagination and social virtues. The fictional story is one of the more hospitable environments for thinking of things as possibly being so. Alasdair MacIntyre has argued that the ability to follow stories is connected with the ability to make sense of human experience because our lives are intelligible only within narratives. Observing that "man is in his actions and practice, as well as in his fictions, essentially a story-telling animal" (1981, p. 201), he points out a complexity of our fiction-making. It is not merely a mode of entertainment but is complicit in how we make sense of ourselves and how we behave as social animals:

> There is no way to give us an understanding of any society, including our own, except through the stock of stories which constitute its initial dramatic resources. Mythology, in its original sense, is at the heart of things. Vico was right and so was Joyce. And so too of course is that moral tradition from heroic stories to its medieval heirs according to which the telling of stories has a key part in educating us into the virtues. (1981, p. 201)

Stories are good for "educating us into the virtues" because the story not only conveys information and describes events and actions but because it also engages our emotions. From earliest times on, the power of stories to engage, and to engage the commitment of, their hearers has been clear. And it is that power that has made some wary or fearful of them, particularly in educating the young. The powerful stories of the world do not simply describe a range of human qualities: they make us somehow a part of those qualities. They hold up for us, and draw us into, thinking and feeling what it would be like to make those qualities a part of our selves. In this way stories are the tool we have for showing others what it is like to feel like we do and for us to find out what it is like to feel as others do. The story, in short, is "the ability to exchange experiences" (Benjamin, 1969, p. 83). Such stories become, simply, a part of us; as Robert Coles writes, quoting one of his students: "in a story — oh, like it says in the Bible, *the word became flesh*" (Coles, 1989, p. 128).

By imaginatively feeling what it would be like to be other than oneself, one begins to develop a prerequisite for treating others with as much respect as one treats oneself. Prejudice — in the religious, class, or racial forms in which we see it so commonly — may be seen in part at least as a failure of imaginative development.

The story's power to contribute to tolerance and a sense of justice needs to be balanced, of course, with its power to do the opposite as well. If the story is one of, say, Aryan superiority and a

Nazi salvation, then it presents another possibility and can lead to quite the opposite of toleration and social justice.

What is the protection against this kind of abuse? There seem to me two. The more trivial, recommended by Plato and so many others since, is that we be careful to tell the right kind of stories to children. The more important protection comes from the stimulation of the imagination by a rich and varied stock of stories, encouraging greater flexibility in thinking of things as possibly being so. Vulnerability to stories like that of the Nazi's is a result, in part at least, of a mind unfamiliar with, and unsophisticated by, the stock of stories that constitute the culture's resources. The value of familiarity with the stock of stories and the kind of sophistication it brings is that one can understand the fictiveness of stories, that they are about possibilities not actualities. The Nazi story is compelling only to people who are poor at understanding fictions and how they work. Not that this is an easy lesson, yielding tidy distinctions between our fictions and reality, but the degree to which we become familiar with the range of stories available in our culture, to that degree we inoculate ourselves against confusing fiction and reality.

Literature is most commonly assumed to be the part of the curriculum in which we become acquainted with some of the great stories of our culture. Proponents of the educational value of literary studies also commonly argue that they can lead to social virtues. Northrop Frye certainly makes this argument eloquently. After demonstrating various ways in which literature stimulates and develops the imagination, he concludes:

> One of the most obvious uses [of imagination] is its encourage-
> ment of tolerance. In the imagination our own beliefs are also
> only possibilities, but we can also see the possibilities in the beliefs
> of others....what produces the tolerance is the power of
> detachment in the imagination, where things are removed just
> out of reach of belief and action. (1963, p. 32)

While literature undoubtedly has such a role in encouraging some social virtues, I think we tend to forget that among the great stories of our culture are those expressed in our science and mathematics and history, among others. Mathematics and science can, if imaginatively taught, build a narrative which provides the student with a context within which the student's life and self become objects to be understood like other objects in the world. The narrative of our science can also contribute importantly to that "detachment in the imagination" that can lead to tolerance and justice.

This way of putting it may seem rather remote from daily activity in the classroom. How can one make today's lesson on exponents or eels contribute to students' social virtues? It can help if we reflect on where exponents or eels fit into the human story of which students are a part. To do this we need to ensure that exponents or eels are not taught as one of a set of algorithms or discrete pieces of knowledge, but that always, however briefly, we tie knowledge in with the human passions, hopes or fears which attended its invention or discovery in the first place, or which account for its continuing human value. We can also contribute towards the end of encouraging social virtues by displaying appropriate modesty, uncertainty, or even bewilderment when teaching. We often present knowledge to students as certain, secure, unquestionable. By presenting it as our best understanding at the moment, or as relatively insecure, or as one possibility, we can encourage students' sense that the world their growing knowledge is enabling them to construct is not Truth or Reality, but one of a number of ways of making sense of the world and experience. Such an attitude towards knowledge encourages open-mindedness and tolerance towards other views. Such an attitude does not commit us to relativism or the belief that all knowledge is socially constructed; rather it simply recommends appropriate epistemological modesty in the classroom.

Imagination and Freedom

We saw in the previous chapter that the earliest stories of the Hebrew and Greek traditions associated the imagination with acts of disobedience that aimed to enlarge or led to enlarging human powers, in particular the power to imagine and plan a future different from the past. This sense of being able to see possibilities beyond the actual and so to make choices and to make the world more nearly like what one's heart desires, has long been considered central to whatever it is in human beings that makes us feel freer than we assume animals or vegetables are. Their lives seem more determined or conditioned by their genetic heritage and their environment. We too are similarly constrained, of course, but nevertheless believe that there is some part of us that can plan and shape our behaviour in ways that allow us to feel some element of freedom

At a trivial level this is evident in daydreaming. I may imagine myself taller, handsomer, richer, more powerful, stronger even than I already am — a prodigious feat of imagination in the Walter Mitty tradition. No doubt some genetic defect or early environmental deprivation may predispose me to this kind of daydreaming, but I can choose to be blond in my daydream rather than dark, or rather than bald. The sense of freedom in these choices may be in some degree illusory. Whether it is or not, it remains a capacity connected with our ability to imagine a different future and to plan and bring about the conditions for that different future. Being able to change the world around us in ways we find desirable and satisfactory is clearly an important capacity. It is what gives us our sense of freedom, illusory or not, and we sensibly value it. As it is a capacity whose strength or weakness turns on the strength or weakness of our imaginations, then clearly we will want to strengthen our imaginations in order to enhance our sense of freedom and enhance the powers that go with it. A well-developed imagination enables us to feel, in Coleridge's nice phrase, unsubdued by habit, unshackled by custom.

"Imagination is what allows us to envision possibilities in or beyond the actualities in which we are immersed" is how Hanson sums up Sartre's general claim about the imagination's role in our sense of freedom (1988, p. 138). We have many accounts by survivors of appalling catastrophes and conditions which eloquently give credit for their survival to their envisioning possibilities beyond those in which they were immersed. Prisoners, and particularly concentration camp survivors, have consistently given witness that, despite the most terrible constraints, powerful imaginations can preserve a vivifying sense of mental freedom.

"Freedom" tends to have meaning only in the context of particular constraints. Of particular interest in education are the constraints associated with the disciplines that have been developed for trying to secure reliable images of reality. The imagination will be productive as well as free when its probing of possibilities is tied with the desire to conceive of the world as it really is. That is, physics, mathematics and history, for example, are not disciplines to be learned separately from our imaginative growth. The imagination has to grow *in* these disciplines, so that their grasp on the world is enriched with meaning, and so that it can recognize and work within the grasp the disciplines can gain on reality.

Imagination and Objective Knowledge

Imagination is commonly considered quite distinct from whatever mental acts are involved in our attempts to gain objective knowledge. The sense of imagination articulated above, however, seems to lead to the conclusion that quite the opposite is the case. The imagination thus should more properly be seen as one of our major tools in the pursuit of objective knowledge, and indeed as establishing the very conditions of objectivity.

One route to justifying this still uncommon view may be taken through a point Ruth Mock makes:

> In the arts and sciences creative imagination demands that an individual frees himself from his immediate preoccupations and associates himself with the medium he is using — the paint, wood, or stone for the painter or sculptor, the words for the writer, the sounds for the musician or the facts for the scientist — so that with it he creates a new form which may to some extent be unexpected even to himself. (1970, p. 21)

What is important here is the observation about the imagination's capacity to inhabit, as it were, the external objects with which it engages, to think what it might be like to be stone or wood being carved. We may see ourselves as distinct beings carving stone, say. But the experienced carver with a well-educated imagination mentally extends into the material being worked, knowing what it is like to break here rather than there, how a stroke here will sheer away whatever is below, and so on. That is, the imaginative sculptor — or mathematician or historian or whatever — becomes in a curious sense one with the materials he or she is working. They feel in high degree something of what Michael Polanyi has described as a part of "tacit knowledge" (Polanyi, 1967) — we feel through the tools and objects we work with; they become extensions of our senses and as such can be incorporated into our imaginations. And it is not just that the stone, say, becomes an extension of ourselves, but that we become an extension of the stone; our minds conform with the nature of the objects that they seek to incorporate, whether those objects are stone and paint, or mathematical symbols, or historical events, or astrophysical phenomena. The world is not objects out there; in as far as we can know the world it is within us by means of that curiously reciprocal arrangement whereby we also extend ourselves imaginatively into it.

So, when learning the geography of Canada or Peru, or about exponents or eels, we do not simply "internalize" information about an "external" world. The disciplines we learn become a part of us; we extend ourselves imaginatively into mathematical or historical or biological worlds and kinds of understanding. We learn to think in particular ways of what was or is possibly true. The disciplines are our tools for trying to grasp — truly — various aspects of reality. So, while imagination can help us to be tolerant and appropriately modest in our claims on knowledge, it also helps us to grasp for a truth or reality that is not subject to our interests, hopes, fears, or intentions. How then can we, in the everyday classroom, try to meet the requirements of imagination's role in developing social virtues, some features of which require skepticism about claims to secure knowledge? Or about its role in trying to uncover a reality which is not subject to skepticism? Precisely by stimulating the imagination's power to conceive of the possible, which enables us on the one hand to remain unshackled by custom and uncommitted to the certainty of what we believe to be the case, and on the other to believe that it is possible to grasp knowledge that is more secure and general than that offered by our own particular viewpoint and interests. Such a power to deal with the ambivalences of our claims to knowledge may, again, seem remote from our lessons on exponents or eels. I think rather that our stance with regard to the knowledge we teach is one crucial variable in making it comprehensible and engaging to students. Later I will take up the unlikely topic of eels and try to show how this principle, among others, can help shape our teaching.

Visualization, Originality, and Creativity

These three topics are being squeezed together into a single brief section because they are kinds of imaginative activity about which much has been written and about whose importance to education there is little argument. Indeed, I will only comment on the first topic.

Ted Hughes has observed that "the word imagination usually denotes not much more than the faculty of creating a picture of something in our heads and holding it there while we think about it" (1988, p. 35). This common, restricted sense of imagination denotes a faculty that can be developed by practice, and that has already been incorporated into various techniques of educational value. The teacher can encourage students to form mental images of whatever is the subject of a lesson, concentrate on the images, elaborate them or move them, and then turn to writing or experimenting or whatever is the appropriate activity. This kind of visualization has found favour in the use of the technique commonly called Guided Imagery. As the name suggests, the images are stimulated by the teacher's descriptions, and the students follow a verbal account that details sights, sounds, tastes, and smells, creating for themselves as vivid images as they can. Students can be encouraged to employ this kind of visualizing on their own to achieve a better grasp on whatever area of knowledge is being dealt with. Perhaps the area of most intensive use of visualizing, and certainly of its most generally accepted effectiveness, has been in sports training to enhance performance. Athletes are encouraged to visualize vividly their intended performance, letting the body rehearse, if only in minimal form, the moves being imagined. The results in terms of improved performance have encouraged educationalists to import the technique into teacher pre-service and in-service programmes.

This capacity clearly overlaps with that reported by Shepard in his account of scientists' and mathematicians' "breakthroughs", and is the subject of much of Shepard's and Kosslyn's empirical research. To see this as paradigmatic of imaginative activity, given the discussion above, would be improper, but to see it as a species of thinking of the possible is obviously sensible. It also overlaps with creativity and originality, both logically, as extensions of thinking of the possible, and empirically, as evident in cases such as Einstein's where visualizing led to his theories of relativity.

The importance of originality and creativity to education, and their close relationship with imagination, needs no further argument, I am assuming.

The Narrative Mind

Brian Sutton-Smith's stark claim that "the mind is...a narrative concern" (1988, p. 22) expresses a view that is becoming increasingly widely accepted. It confronts the long-assumed view that the mind is, when functioning productively and properly, a logical concern working with abstract concepts. Reason was thus taken as evident only in limited logical operations. Increasingly these operations are seen as themselves grounded in and growing out of narrative and metaphoric bases (Lakoff & Johnson, 1980; Langer, 1967, 1972, 1982; Kolakowski, 1989). When someone could talk of a parent's reasonless love for a child, the sense of reason was restricted to what could be demonstrated in something like a formal logical fashion. A parent's love for a child is entirely reasonable, once we rescue "reason" from the prison it has been in and reconnect it to the imagination. Without this connection it is dessicated and closer to a form of calculation than to the richness and complexity of human reason as it operates in the narratives of our lives.

As it becomes clearer that the mind functions as a whole and that this whole includes our bodies, then the sense of the mind as an elaborate calculating organ with reason as its mode of calculating becomes increasingly untenable. It becomes clear that rationality is not a set of skills one can train but is rather tied up with all these hitherto neglected attics, basements, and hidden rooms of the mind, in which emotions, intentions, metaphors, and the imagination cavort. And so it has been rediscovered that we make sense of the world and of our experience in narratives, that we can recall items in narrative structures better than in logically organized lists, that we more profoundly code knowledge in our memories by affective than by logical associations, that young children deal more readily and flexibly with metaphor than do older, schooled children, and so on and on.

The rediscovery of the narrative mind encourages us to pay more attention to imagination because the imagination is more evident in the composition of narratives and their construction of possibilities. Learning to follow narratives is thus seen to involve the development of more significant intellectual capacities than has traditionally been recognized. In particular, to quote Northrop Frye, "The art of listening to stories is a basic training for the imagination" (1963, p. 49). The ability to follow stories stimulates and develops the narrative mode of the mind and its sense-making, meaning-making capacities. Many and varied stories can help to make more sophisticated our grasp on, and use of, metaphor, which is itself the connecting logic of narrative and a central component in the causality which holds stories together. The causality of stories involves both logical and emotional components together. That is, in stories the sequencing of events that are intelligible, that make sense, is not simply logical, though it has to be so in part, but it involves as well an affective pattern. We jump from, say, the scene where Cinderella sees the sisters off to the ball to that in which the Fairy Godmother arrives. Following a purely logical causal sequence we might have to witness some dish-washing or dusting or coal-heaving or whatever, but the affective causality makes the connection between the two scenes immediate and directly comprehensible. Learning to follow stories is to develop these mental capacities, to make more flexible our manipulation of possibilities. As they become more developed, even works like

James Joyce's *Ulysses* and *Finnegans Wake* become comprehensible, and those sophistications of narrative comprehension become available for making sense of our own experience and of the world we find ourselves in.

The development of the narrative capacities of the mind, of its ready use of metaphor, of its integration of cognitive and affective, of its sense-making and meaning-making, and of its overarching imagination, is of educational importance because these capacities are so central to our *general* capacity to make meaning out of experience. Our lives are "understood as embodying a certain type of narrative structure" (MacIntyre, 1981, p. 163). Any event or behaviour has no meaning by itself; it "becomes intelligible by finding its place in a narrative" (MacIntyre, 1981, p. 196). Barbara Hardy puts it emphatically: "We dream in narrative, daydream in narrative, remember, anticipate, hope, despair, believe, doubt, plan, revise, criticize, construct, gossip, learn, hate and live by narrative" (1968, p. 5).

So, in as far as we want the world to be intelligible to students and in as far as we value the elements of the list Barbara Hardy gives us above, the stimulation and development of the narrative mode of mind is educationally important. And this mode, born out of stories to help us remember, is the domain in which the imagination is indispensable.

Developing the narrative mode of the mind tends to receive less emphasis in schools because it is not seen to be productive, in the way that developing logico-mathematical skills is seen to be productive. The utilitarian role of schools communicates itself to children very readily. Nearly all children when asked why they go to school reply "To get a job" (Cullingford, 1991). Frye notes that "Every child realizes that literature is taking him [or her] in a different direction from the immediately useful, and a good many children complain loudly about this" (1963, p. 2). Imagination takes us increasingly into a world where possibility, contingency, the conditional and provisional surround the actual, and draw us away from unadorned literal actuality. One role of education is to clarify for children that the life of the imagination offers rewards that may not seem immediately useful but that are nonetheless worthwhile. And, most significantly for education, access to narratives seems possible for everyone, literate or not, and they provide an obvious route to all kinds of knowledge. Educators might wisely develop "a respect for narrative as everyone's rock-bottom capacity, but also as the universal gift, to be shared with others" (Coles, 1989, p. 30).

Conclusion

I have included a wide range of features in this attempt to sketch some reasons why imagination is important to education. Perhaps you might feel that I have included too much and that the result is a sense of imagination being involved in everything of educational importance. Such a reading would not mistake my intention, but I would want to argue that this sense would not include too much. Indeed, I think imagination should properly be very pervasive in education. Such a view is difficult to take only if we think of imagination as a thing, as a particular, distinct part of the mind. If we see it rather as a particular kind of flexibility, energy, and vividness that comes from the ability to think of the possible and not just the actual and which can imbue all mental functions, then its role in all the topics I have mentioned above becomes easier to understand. To be imaginative, then, is not to have a particular function highly developed, but it is to have heightened capacity in all mental functions. It is not, in particular, something distinct from reason, but rather it is what gives reason flexibility, energy, and vividness. It makes all mental life more meaningful; it makes life more abundant. John Dewey expressed this sense of the pervasiveness of imagination this way: "Imagination is as much a normal and integral part of human activity as is muscular movement" (1966, p. 237).

CHAPTER THREE

Characteristics of Students' Imaginative Lives, Ages 8-15

Introduction

So far we have been considering the imagination in general, trying to bring together a sense of its pervasiveness in thinking and its potential value to education. While we might now have a better grasp on imagination than has been common in educational discourse, and reasons to take it more seriously in educational practice than has been usual, there remain some obstacles in the way of direct implementation. There are technical problems in how one might go about developing imagination with a typical class of students while teaching the typical content required by governmental curriculum documents, and there is also a particular theoretical problem.

The theoretical problem derives from the observation that imagination, like our bodies and other intellectual characteristics, is subject to age- and experience-related changes. The imaginative life of the typical five year old has characteristics that are significantly unlike those of the typical fifteen year old. There are obviously some common features, but equally obviously some differences. When teaching, it would not be sensible to try engaging the five year old's imagination with approaches and material better suited to the fifteen year old, and vice versa. Consequently, before we can design suitable techniques and planning frameworks for engaging, stimulating, and developing the imaginations of students between eight and fifteen, we must descend, as it were, one step down from the generalizations of the previous chapter and try to see what particular forms those general characteristics take in the imaginative lives of typical students today.

How can we go about this? This is not an area in which we can turn to empirical research for much help. Empirical research can usefully come into play once the phenomena to be dealt with are clearly conceptualized — but this has so far been lacking for imagination. What I will do here, then, is try to describe some fairly general characteristics of students' imaginations. That is, if imagination is being able to think of things as possibly being so, what are some of the prominent features of the possible worlds students in this age-range construct? This chapter will be exploratory, using the concept of imagination developed above and attempting to establish some generalizations that can then be used in the following chapters to design teaching techniques. The approach here has to be exploratory because this kind of characterization of imagination is not common in education: there is very little research to draw on, much of the literature uses diffuse and varied concepts of imagination, and the abundant studies of students' games, reading, social activities, and so on, rarely move towards generalizations about students' imaginations such as I am seeking here.

The results of this exploration, then, will not be of the kind that follow elaborate empirical research studies. But, even so, they will have a firm, and I think largely uncontentious, empirical basis. I will return to this in the conclusion to the chapter, where discussion of the nature of the generalizations reached will be more meaningful. The studies of students' reading, games, social activities, and so on, while usually framed quite differently from what follows in this chapter, do form a useful background on which I have drawn. On the whole, however, it seems most economical to elaborate the characteristics of students' imaginations relying very largely on the kinds of uncontentious observations which any parent or teacher can make. So, to simplify a little, I am giving two reasons for the rather unusual procedure of making a range of empirical generalizations about students' imaginations while not supplying the kinds of supporting references that are common. First, there are none and, second, they are anyway unnecessary given the nature of the claims. But let us revisit this in the conclusion.

I recognize that bunching together students from about age eight to about age fifteen will seem odd. This is the period of life during which we seem to go through the greatest physical, emotional, and intellectual changes, and all developmental theories mark out significant stage divisions within this age group. But the choice of years, while obviously allowing for considerable individual variation at each end, is not arbitrary. I have been driven to it not by some theoretical assumptions but by the kind of data I have been dealing with. While clearly students' imaginative lives go through changes and developments within this age-range — some of which I will refer to in what follows — there do seem sufficient common features to justify this general "romantic" categorization. Also one should not read such attempted segmenting and categorizing of what is after all a continually changing developmental process too rigidly. Such categories are simply heuristic devices to help us focus on particular aspects of development. It just so happens that the common features in students' imagination that I focus on seem to persist across this age range. I suppose the best justification for this unusual segmenting will come from parents and teachers who acknowledge that they do see these characteristics in students at eight and at fifteen and between these years. I will refer below to the kinds of reading, games, T.V. shows and stories that are frequently enjoyed by this age-range, and try to add informal justification for the category by such references. A tighter form of empirical research than has justified creating the category can then be brought to bear on testing it. But, again, conceptualization has to precede such research.

The Affective Connection

Since Hume's observations that lively passions attend a lively imagination and that there is a close connection between the imagination and our affective states, it has become a commonplace of studies of the imagination to note its ties to our emotions. Sartre even suggests a criterion for distinguishing between an image generated from the memory and one generated from the imagination: the latter *always* evokes an affective condition. The connection is also reflected in the wisdom of earliest times: oral cultures tied their lore to vivid images and wrapped it in stories that could organize affective responses to it. Taking White's more austere conclusion, the connection is evident when we consider that what drives us to think of things as possibly being so is our hopes, fears, and intentions.

MacIntyre's observation that we are essentially a story-telling animal is accurate because we are an animal with the kinds of affective lives that we have. Our relations with the world around us, and our manner of making sense of our experience, are profoundly mediated by our emotions. MacIntyre's point about the narrative shape of our lives is true *only* because of how we feel about, and feel during, the sequences of our lives. Birth, growth, maturity, and death, as Northrop Frye has argued, provide a pattern for our narratives (1957).

So the affective connection is also the story connection. Whenever our emotions are involved, so too is a narrative, a story or story fragment, that sets the context and the meaning. The role of the story is fundamental to our sense-making, and, in education where sense-making is of primary concern, it is still largely neglected. "Story" does not necessarily imply a fictional narrative; rather it involves the narrative shaping of any content.

So, a first evident characteristic of students' imaginative lives is that they are readily engaged by stories. Remembering Sutton-Smith's point about the mind being a narrative concern, might encourage us to think of lessons and units as good stories to be told rather than as blocks of knowledge to be sorted, graded, and sequenced for "effective" teaching. If instead we think of *affective* teaching of narratives which tell the imaginatively engaging stories of our physics, history, mathematics, and so on, then we will see our way to an alternative form of planning and teaching. What leads us to this conclusion is the uncontentious observation that students' imaginations are more readily stimulated by content that engages their emotions than by content that doesn't. The tool we have for dealing with knowledge and emotions together is the story.

But as the imagination goes through age- and experience-related changes, so too do the characteristics of the narratives that students find engaging. The kind of story that is most engaging to the typical five year old will not usually be so engaging to the typical fifteen year old. For the observation about the importance of the story to be converted to practical use in teaching, it is necessary to be more particular about the characteristics of the kinds of stories that eight to fifteen year olds are engaged by. Or, put more generally, as the story is the narrative unit that carries its context with it, it is the kinds of contexts within which eight to fifteen year olds find knowledge meaningful that it is necessary to be more precise about.

We can first note that the story structure that engages the older group is more complex than that which appeals to younger children, and so we will expect the structure of any planning techniques derived from it to be different from that which I have described for the younger age group (Egan, 1986). Also developments in literacy bring with them other intellectual tools for making sense of the world and of experience, which reduce somewhat the prominence of the story form for students in the eight-to-fifteen age group. This is not a contradiction of the emphasis laid above on the importance of the story. Rather, the story and the narrative shaping of content is emphasized because it remains important and because it is so commonly neglected or undervalued; at least its implications are rarely attended to. But it is increasingly less dominant than it seems to be before age eight. So, in designing a planning technique we will want to give appropriate emphasis to the need for our lessons and units to have a narrative structure, but it will not appear so prominent as it needs to be for younger children.

What I will do in the following sections of this chapter is discuss a set of more particular characteristics of the narratives that engage students' imaginations during these years. In addition I will discuss characteristics which are imaginatively engaging but in which the narrative component is less prominent. The main conclusion from this discussion of "the affective connection", however, is that if we wish to engage students' imaginations we need to attend to engaging their emotions, and to engage their emotions we need to attend to story or narrative structuring. So, even though some of the following characteristics might seem to engage the imagination without being embedded in a narrative, I am suggesting that by providing a narrative context for them we can enhance their power to stimulate and develop the imagination.

Extremes and Limits

Even the most casual observation of the kind of knowledge that most readily engages students' imaginations during these years shows that it is about the extremes and limits of human experience and the natural world: the most courageous or the cruellest acts, the strangest and the most bizarre natural phenomena, the most terrible or the most wonderful events. These are staples of the T.V. shows, books, and films that exploit this prominent characteristic of students' imaginations. (That such shows or books also appeal to so many adults is no objection to my point. These characteristics do not go away as we grow older. They may change in certain ways, but the appeal of extremes and limits remains common to much of the adult population.) *The Guinness Book of Records* is a most successful exploiter of this particular characteristic, as are those T.V. shows that explore mysteries of nature or amazing achievements.

A notable feature of this very evident characteristic of early adolescents' imaginations is how little it has influenced educational discourse. Indeed, the commonest lore and literature about "where the students are" do not just ignore it but assume that something like the opposite is the case. That is, to repeat the point made earlier, it seems more commonly assumed that students' imaginations can be primarily engaged by knowledge of local environments and familiar experiences. If you have to teach a class of twelve year olds and want to engage their interest readily, and have two topics to choose between — "Important features of your neighbourhood" and "Torture instruments through the ages" —

which do you think would go down best? (This is not a curriculum recommendation!) That the latter is most readily engaging points to a principle which is commonly ignored.

I am suggesting that the more distant and different something is from students' everyday experience and environments, the more imaginatively engaging it is likely to be. But I should be more careful how I put this. I am in danger of trying to emphasize what seems to me a very important and neglected point in a way that then underestimates or seems to deny how the local and immediate also serves in stimulating students' imaginations. What seems to happen when students are engaged by knowledge of some exotic phenomenon or some amazing event is that a kind of dialectical process comes into play. The exotic or amazing knowledge is understood in terms of what is already known from the students' everyday experience, while at the same time the exotic new knowledge forces the student to understand everyday experience a little differently. Relatedly, we can find the local and immediate imaginatively engaging when we suddenly see what we had taken for granted as itself strange or different in some way. So my point is not that the students' everyday experience is irrelevant to their imaginative engagements. Rather I want to point out that the assumption that everyday experience must be a *starting point* for engaging the imagination can be profoundly misleading. It is, of course, vital, but it plays a role in stimulating the imagination when it is engaged dialectically with knowledge that is most different and distant. So emphasis on extremes and limits does not remove us from everyday experience, but enables us to see it in a new light.

The fascination with the extremes of reality and the limits of experience during the years from about eight to fifteen seems to be a part of an orientation process. Students are interested in limits and extremes because such exotica provide the context within which their daily lives and experience are meaningful. By establishing the limits, we can get a proportionate sense of the local and everyday; we learn where the familiar fits, what its meaning is. So what sometimes seems to some teachers as a regrettable fascination with exotic trivia, is in fact a profoundly sensible strategy for making sense of one's place in the scheme of things.

Only by knowing the limits and extremes of things can we make sense of our place. It is worth remembering that our sense of ourselves has been most affected during the last couple of centuries not by psychology or those sciences that focus on our selves and our everyday lives and environments, but by those sciences that have dealt with exotic and distant stuff, like our location in the galaxy, the size of the universe, the evolution of species, the age and changing structure of the earth, and so on.

The point of this for teaching techniques for this age group is that we will need to build in some ways of routinely involving extremes and limits in whatever we teach. I will show some ways we can do this in the next couple of chapters. But this is not a requirement that every class focus on the bizarre and exotic all the time. It is important to remember the dialectic that runs between limits and extremes and the everyday, and that the everyday itself can be seen as exhibiting some limits and extremes when viewed in a new light. Indeed, as we shall see, *anything* can engage this characteristic of students' imaginations if seen in an appropriate perspective.

A further point worth mentioning here, but relevant throughout, is that there are some obvious differences between male and female imaginative engagements during these years. The differences tend to become more marked as the years go by. The main characteristics I will note in this chapter seem to me common to both sexes, even if they typically find expression in somewhat different forms and contents. Some of these characteristics, however, seem typically stronger in males and some stronger in females. This particular engagement with limits and extremes may seem somewhat more prominent in males than in females, though I suspect it seems so only because of the way I have exemplified it. If I had emphasized a bit more the compassionate engagement with distinct forms of experience and the imaginative sympathy necessary for understanding them — which are central features of this characteristic — then it might be more apparently a female characteristic. Regardless of how it is illustrated, the importance of this characteristic in the imaginative lives of both males and females during these years seems clear, and significantly neglected in education. The task ahead is to recognize its importance for developing techniques that can be readily employed in everyday teaching.

Romance, Wonder, and Awe

The archetypal romance is the heroic journey in which a Sir Galahad braves dangers and encounters wonders and varied adventures in pursuit of some noble but ineffable Holy Grail. The general archetype of the heroic journey can be fitted to many varied situations and events. By seeing other situations and events as heroic journeys, even if the archetype is not at all overt, we heighten their significance and enhance their meaning. So we can tell the story of Florence Nightingale's struggles to introduce professional nursing not just as a series of particular historical events, but as a powerfully plotted tale that embodies the hidden romantic archetype.

The archetype itself can remain hidden because it is so familiar to us that we notice it only if it is drawn to our attention, or if it is embodied in a crude or inappropriate way. Used appropriately, though, it can reveal Florence Nightingale not only as the flesh and blood woman she was, but also as one engaged on an heroic journey, moving towards a noble goal through many adversities. Such an archetype organizes our emotional responses to Florence Nightingale's struggles and to those who helped or opposed her. In so plotting her story, we need not falsify anything, but we can heighten the significance of the events and enhance their meaning. Certainly we are enabled to make clearer sense of the complex events of her life by thinking about their possibly being so in terms of the archetype.

The capacity to heighten significance and enlarge meaning by thinking about events "romantically" can be applied not just to great people doing great deeds. Such great achievers obviously provide the easiest application of the romantic archetype; we tend to organize our knowledge of them into this pattern almost without thinking. But there seems almost no limit to what we can apply it to. This discovery — that we can heighten significance and enlarge meaning by thinking about events or things as possibly fitting some archetypal plot — is something which was enormously developed by the Romantic poets.

The sense of the heroic could be seen not just in a Napoleon leading his soldiers over the storm-tossed Alps to martial victories for the greater glory of France but also, as Wordsworth showed most powerfully, in leech-gatherers or in farmers or in all kinds of everyday people. But Wordsworth went further and saw that by focussing a romantic enlargement of meaning on the everyday world around him, the everyday too could be enriched, enhanced, and shown to be wonderful. So this path, these trees, this season of the year, those daffodils could be thought about not just as themselves but as things embodying much greater significance. We can think about universes in grains of sand, forests in a handful of seeds, wonder and mystery in a stone or shell. The stone or the daffodils become heroic in that they are thought of as partners in our journey through time and space towards greater understanding or truer feeling.

The Romantic poets wrote mostly about the details of their everyday world. They domesticated the sense of romance that had earlier been evoked by the likes of Sir Galahad or the heroic achievements of a David fighting Goliath, or tiny Athens defeating the army of the huge Persian Empire. They greatly developed, and we have inherited the potential to develop, an imaginative capacity to think about almost any feature of the life and of the world in romantically heightened terms, as possibly fitting the romantic archetype.

By focussing on — to take an extreme and unlikely example — a discarded, broken styrofoam cup, we can think about it not simply as environmentally damaging waste. We can enlarge its significance by considering it as a part of the heroic journey that is the human struggle to shape the world more closely to our desires, to find release from the constant toil, sickness, and pain that have been the lot of most people most of the time. We can see in the almost infinitely reproduced cup an immense ingenuity; we can hold burning liquids in it without our fingers being burned. The knowledge of chemical and physical processes that have gone into its design and making is prodigious. And we have learned the environmental costs entailed in applying this knowledge to create this convenience, and we are as a society recognizing that we must satisfy this particular desire in other ways that do not threaten our harmony with the natural world, and so on. One can flash such thoughts through the mind in less than half a second; one does not compose such meditations verbally in one's head. They are associations that come with the romantic image of the broken cup. Such constant flashes of enlarged significance are the product of the capacity to think about anything romantically; they occur as the imagination holds an object as possibly fitting in this perspective.

The emotion most commonly generated by this romantic highlighting of things is wonder. The broken cup ceases to be merely a piece of useless garbage and becomes briefly an object of wonder. Wonder is generated by our perceiving something as extraordinary, as rare and strange. The imaginative capacity developed along with a heightened sense of romance enables us to think about anything and everything as wonderful. This is a capacity that can greatly enrich our lives; at its fullest development we may feel that raising of our spirits which W. B. Yeats captures in sensing that "everything we look upon is bless'd".

We are, I recognize, some way from the typical social-studies worksheet or mathematics test, and it is important not to lose touch with them or with the everyday rumble of the typical classroom. I am taking time to characterize romance and wonder, and will go on to consider awe, because I want to suggest that these years are particularly suitable for their development and that, when we look at typical students' imaginative engagements, we will find these characteristics already evident.

Also, parenthetically, recognizing the capacity to think about anything as wonderful helps further to expose what is wrong with the prevailing assumption that we have to begin introducing new knowledge by starting with content that is familiar in students' everyday experience. The argument moves through the following steps: everyday experience and familiar content must be made meaningful in an enriched way; this comes about by thinking of it as wonderful; this capacity is a product of developing the sense of romance; the sense of romance is initially most readily engaged, stimulated, and developed by heroic and exotic figures such as Sir Galahad, Florence Nightingale, hobbits, princesses and Star Warriors; we can then focus our developing sense of romance on the everyday and familiar and think about our daily lives as wonderful, as heroic journeys. The argument, that is, leads us to one of those paradoxes; it is by focussing on the distant and strange that we can enlarge the meaning of the familiar world around us.

Currently in North America, partly no doubt as a result of the peculiar uses of English common among U.S. politicians, the term "awesome" has become a general term of approval among students, ("radically awesome" being the preferred superlative). Wonder and awe are often used as synonyms, but I think it is worth trying to preserve a distinction between them. Wonder, again, is the emotion evoked by perceiving something as extraordinary or strange, or as an extreme achievement. It is concerned with the real world, and most readily picks out those features of it that are most rare. Awe, on the other hand, is the emotion evoked by the perception that beyond or behind or beneath the real, tangible world around us we are adrift in an ocean of mystery. Wonder may be evoked by contemplating the remarkable powers of this sophisticated computer sitting here on my desk; awe may be evoked by the sudden bewilderment that the computer and desk and I exist at all. Awe is the sense of the mystery that underlies existence; it is evoked by a vivid awareness of all that lies beyond our comprehension, beyond thinking about, and beyond explaining. It is connected with a sense of the miraculous. Contemplating the near-infinity of chance events that brought about the universe as we know it and the earth as we know it, may stimulate wonder; awe derives from what is beyond the calculable, the contemplatable, the search for lawful patterns — it derives ultimately from facing the mystery of why there is existence rather than non-existence. Students might first make contact with it while contemplating infinity — in numbers or space or time.

Awe may not seem like a very useful kind of emotion, relying as it does on what may seem like a very un-useful kind of perception. But it seems fundamental to understanding, and being able to deal with, the contingency of things. A person familiar with awe is less likely to be a victim of surprise at the way life happens to clobber out events. It provides an even wider context than does knowledge of the limits and extremes of reality for enabling us to ascribe meaning to the details of our lives and the world around us.

Romance, wonder, and awe seem to go through their most intense development during the eight-to-fifteen-year-old period. No doubt, as various psycho-sexual theories proclaim, some of the development of these capacities is connected with puberty. (I try to give additional reasons in Egan, 1990.) But here I am less concerned with trying to explain, and more with trying to describe, these capacities. Above, then, I have tried to characterize them in rather general terms. What remains is to show that we can find these characteristics prominently at work when students' imaginations are engaged by materials of their choice. I will do this briefly here and, in the following sections, which overlap with and elaborate aspects of these characteristics, I will add further examples.

If we examine the kinds of books and comics which students choose to read during this period, features of romance are clearly prominent. The attraction to the exotic and extraordinary is evident in the pervasive adventure stories, whether they are the more male-oriented star-warrior or Super Hero type, or the more female-oriented Witch or Spy type. Even in the domestic adventures of T.V. shows or Archie comics or "teen-romances", the highlighting and simplification frees the characters from the complex of everyday concerns that hem us in and shows the central characters transcending the constraints set up within the particular episode or story.

The sense of wonder is similarly evident in T.V. shows or books that focus on strange and bizarre phenomena and experiences. "Mysteries of the Universe" are more engaging to the typical student than explorations of the everyday world. Wonder and romance are clearly connected with the engagement with extremes and limits discussed above. Wonder, in particular, is stimulated most easily by those features of the world and of experience that are, or can be thought of as, strange and exotic. We can see a burgeoning sense of wonder in natural phenomena — the new realization of delight in getting drenched, in the rush of the air, in gaudy sunsets, in spring's quickening. We see it too in a new realization of delight in language — in private codes, in exploring the limits of abuse or slang, in the control over the world which language seems able to provide in diaries.

The sense of awe may seem less evident, but it becomes apparent in early adolescents' not uncommon bewildered fascination with themselves and the curious discovery that they are who they are. Reflections of it may be seen in some students in the development of religious feelings, whether students seek an outlet for these feelings within some organized religion or not. In some more literary students we see it in the writing of poetry, which typically is kept private. I think we also may see aspects of it in the (more commonly female) interest in the supernatural and the half-serious, half-fearful, and half-fun (the three halves being appropriate here!) engagement with such things as ouija boards, tarot cards, palm-reading, and so on. In both sexes, the debased forms of the sense of awe accounts for the attraction of the spooky, the scary, the spine-tingling films or books that suggest a quite different reality lurks just behind or below the surface of the everyday world.

For very many students, because there is little general awareness of awe as a distinct emotion in our culture, we see only sporadic hints of its development. There is hardly any deliberate evocation and stimulation of awe in current curricula; there are no books on teaching techniques that consider how it may be stimulated; there is no clear recognition of its place within education. There are certainly no assessment procedures aimed at its detection.

Associating With the Heroic

The romantic hero does not only become an archetype which we can use to stimulate a capacity for thinking about broken styrofoam cups as possibly being wonderful. A further characteristic of students' imaginative lives during this period involves a more straightforward embodiment of the archetypal hero. But these days students are more likely to identify it in a pop-star or football player than in Florence Nightingale or Sir Galahad.

The hero is a person who lives in the real world, or in a plausible world, and who overcomes the constraints of reality that hem the rest of us in. Particularly between eight and fifteen, students are increasingly recognizing themselves as distinct individuals and sensing their growing powers. But in our society, students of this age are also relatively powerless. They are subject to parents' rules, school rules, and constraints of many kinds everywhere they turn. The hero is someone who is subject to the same kind of rules, but also somehow transcends them. Many of the "teen-exploitation" movies, such as *Ferris Beuhler's Day Off*, or novels, such as *Anne of Green Gables* or its "down-market" kin, feature a character supposedly subject to the same constraints as the students watching or reading. What makes the character heroic is his or her ability to transcend the constraints, and to triumph over all those who represent the constraining forces — parents, teachers, road rules, conventional behaviour, and society in general.

The student watcher or reader associates with the confidence, self-reliance, persistence, energy, ingenuity, and so on, that enables the hero to achieve a delicious sense of freedom, in which the student shares. That is, the student provisionally thinks of herself or himself as embodying the transcendent quality represented in the hero.

Associating with the heroic need not mean associating with male heroes achieving traditional forms of male dominance. This characteristic is an extension of those discussed above. As with those, the hero can be a broken styrofoam cup, Florence Nightingale, a daffodil, or whatever. The important characteristic of students' imaginations is the capacity for associating with the heroic in a way which involves participating in heroism. Students "try on", as it were, the heroic qualities that they admire. We move in the direction of what we admire, as far as we can, and, during this period of self-definition, students commonly admire and move towards a variety of heroic qualities.

Sometimes the admiration may be of the heroic compassion of a mother or the gentleness of a father. A parent can thus be in some degree, some of the time, a hero for a student, as the parent embodies human qualities that transcend everyday constraints and conventions. So the parent is admired and grown towards. Perhaps more commonly, or more publicly, the hero might be a pop-group which embodies a transcendent confidence in their revolt against adult conventions. Students may admire and begin to adopt that confidence and that revolt. The heroic quality might be the serene patience of a cat, the courage of a dog, the technical virtuosity of a pianist or football player, the endurance of an explorer, the tenacity of a weed on a rock face, the sardonic wisdom of a grandparent, or the beauty of a building. The world, to the romantic imagination, is thronged with heroes.

An important point to note about these associations is that they are not primarily with the pop-group or weed or pianist, but are with them only in as far as they embody an heroic, transcendent human quality — the confidence, endurance, revolt against convention, courage, compassion, and so on. Associating with the heroic involves imaginatively inhabiting for a while the transcendent human quality the student admires, or indeed, wonders at.

So, in designing techniques to engage students' imaginations in learning during this period we will want to build in ways to encourage their association with some heroic or transcendent human qualities embodied in the material to be taught.

Revolt and Idealism

The period between eight and fifteen is that during which students realize that the constraining world that hems them in is also their inheritance. It is a period of growing ambivalence, during which students seek "alternately to resist the adult world and to find a place in it" (Spacks, 1981, p. 15).

In the adjustments from powerless dependence to gradually increasing power and independence there are inevitably tensions and conflicts between the growing student and the adult world. It is rarely an entirely smooth transition. The conflicts often display themselves in the adult world's denying the student some freedom that the student wants. This commonly breeds a sense of injustice in the student. The most visible response to this is sporadic revolt against adult norms, conventions, and expectations. In most cases this revolt is not particularly overt or sustained. (Even in the most publicized periods of generational conflict, we may easily forget, the large majority of students identify with the values of their parents [Springhall, 1986].) The forms of revolt are many: from sulking reluctance, to quiet resistance, to flaunting styles of hair, clothing, music and dancing that confront adult conventions and values, to outright refusal to play the adult game or at least that part of it played out in schools.

Revolt implies an ideal, whose absence justifies the revolt. This is the period during which we find students expressing ideals of how the world should work on the one hand, but also experimenting with ideal roles for themselves. Some sense of the ideals which they are forming for themselves become evident as they "try on", think of themselves as possibly embodying, such roles as the confident hero, the serene lady, the rebel, the fashion plate or dandy, the hoyden, the macho, the tease, the socialite, the cool dude, the iceberg, the friendly innocent, and so on. As these behavioural roles are tried on, however tentatively, students also less constrainedly pursue roles for themselves in their fantasizing or daydreaming. So they imagine themselves embodying extremes of power, beauty, daring, influence, nobility, and wealth; saving the planet from wicked polluters; writing great literature; defending the weak and innocent, and so on. In these daydreams are formed ideals, senses of direction, possibilities that provide avenues for movement and action. The imagination is energetically active in all this, thinking through possibilities, probing for what fits the burgeoning self.

How is this rather routine observation supposed to help us in teaching classes in physics or history? It is something of a cliché that students, particularly during early adolescence, develop varied forms of revolt and begin to form ideals, and that these two are connected. That they are also characteristic forms of imaginative activity during this period is hardly contentious. If these common observations are true, then we might look for ways in which these characteristics of students' imaginative lives might be engaged by the typical content of physics or history. I will consider various ways of doing this in the following chapters, but, even at the very crudest level, we can see how the lives of scientists whose discoveries were made only after revolt against prevailing conventions provide students with a sympathetic access to their work. The connection between a scientist's ideals that drove her or him to revolt against conventions also can mirror profound features of students' imaginative experience, and provide the burgeoning revolt and idealism of the student with aliments or models to grow on. What this suggests to us as teachers, again, is the desirability of re-embedding the knowledge we want students to learn in the emotional and imaginative reality from which typical textbooks so unimaginatively rip it.

This does not mean, of course, that we need to try to represent all knowledge to students in terms of ideals and revolt. These are just a couple of related characteristics of students' imaginations during this period — two that tend to become more prominent later in the period. We will want to consider them in light of, and in relation to, the set of other characteristics touched on here, but we would be a bit obtuse not to consider them at all when planning to teach students in whom they are vivid parts of their intellectual lives. If our aim is to recognize "where the students are", we need to bear in mind that "where they are" is a place of increasing idealism, with revolt constantly nudging their elbows.

Matters of Detail

Students during this period, to repeat another cliché, are becoming increasingly aware of a complex real world outside of themselves and their familiar environments. Unlike the extensive fantasy worlds of childhood, this one is real, and knowing about it clearly matters in a pragmatic way. One problem with this world, which we have noted already, is that students have little sense of its extent or limits. Consequently they do not have any clear context for their familiar environments or even for themselves and their lives. As discussed earlier, we discover an important dimension of the meaning of things by discovering the context within which they exist, and the interest in the extremes and limits of reality seems to be propelled by the desire to grasp some of the contexts within which the everyday world and our lives can be better understood.

The imaginative engagement in the extremes, the exotic, the strange is mirrored by another exploration of limits that takes quite a different form. This is an exploration of something in exhaustive detail. It is as though by discovering everything about something we will again get some secure sense of the extent of reality, or at least some part of it. At least, we gain the comfort of realizing that the world is not limitless, and that we can get intellectual control over some aspects of it.

We see this kind of detailed exploration in the obsessive hobbies or collections that reach a peak during this period. By collecting a set — of ornamental spoons, of compact disk recordings by a favourite pop singer, of hockey cards, of dolls, of particular comics, of the books of some author in a uniform edition, of stones or shells, of illustrations of costumes through the ages, of whatever — one gets some secure intellectual hold over something. The set need not be completed, of course, though there is a strong impulse to complete it if possible. But some satisfaction comes in discovering just what the limits of the set are. It remains common, for example, to continue collecting postage stamps despite the fact that one cannot expect to collect an example of all the stamps, even those of one's specialty. (The more specialized one becomes, the more minute variations elaborate greatly what one needs to collect.) But one learns what the limits are, what one would need to complete sets of one's specialization.

So a further characteristic of imaginative engagements during this period is the attempt to get an exhaustive grasp of the details of some area of knowledge. The range of hobbies and things collected by students suggests that the object of this engagement is largely arbitrary. It can be engaged by a very wide range of things, as those who exploit it commercially have shown. The educational task, again, is to plan our teaching in such a way that this characteristic can be engaged by the material of our lessons and units. And yet again, it is surely odd that this very evident, very powerful drive exhibited by nearly all students in one form or another, is very largely ignored in educational theory and research.

Humanizing Knowledge

As any journalist knows, information can be made more engaging if it is given a "human interest" angle. That is, knowledge or information seen through, or by means of, human emotions, actions, hopes, fears, and so on, is not only more directly comprehensible but is also more engaging and meaningful. Every teacher knows how the illustrative anecdote, particularly if it involves extremes of human endurance or foresight or ingenuity or compassion or suffering, grabs students' attention. My purpose is not to recommend this widely recognized technique, but rather is to see it as exemplifying a characteristic of students' imaginations that can have more general and pervasive implications for educational practice.

The structure of typical textbooks with their neatly organized, segmented, sequenced packages of knowledge tends to convey the impression that the textbook, or perhaps the encyclopaedia, exhibits the archetypal form of knowledge. This bizarre idea is no doubt one of the more peculiar consequences of literacy. What needs to be emphasized constantly in education is that books do not contain knowledge. Books contain symbolic codes which serve as a kind of external mnemonic for knowledge. Knowledge exists only in minds. And in minds its meaning derives from the connection with our hopes, fears, intentions, and with our imaginative lives.

By emphasizing the difference between inert symbolic codes in books and living knowledge in human minds, attention is drawn to something significant, and often neglected, about teaching. The point is not to get the symbolic codes as they exist in books into students' minds. We can, of course, do that — training students to be rather ineffective 'copies' of books. Rather, the teaching task is to reconstitute the inert symbolic codes into living human knowledge.

The paradigm of knowledge is that which is meaningful and vital in human minds. Symbolic codes in books are a very clever way of preserving in suspended animation, as it were, some aspects of this living knowledge. Yet so much educational practice assumes that the textbook's symbolic codes represent the paradigmatic form of knowledge with which students' minds must be made to conform. Assessment techniques that require students to reproduce symbolic codes rather than give evidence that they have made the knowledge meaningful, simply encourage this travesty of education.

The educational task involves the resuscitation of knowledge from its suspended animation in symbolic codes. The task is to convert, re-animate, transmute the symbolic codes into living human knowledge in students' minds. When we see the task this way, our emphasis is on *meaning*. And in addition, we see that a primary tool necessary for this transmutation from codes to living knowledge is the imagination — the students' capacity to think about the decoded content as part of some possible human world. And, drawing on points made earlier, knowledge embedded in the context of people's lives — those who invented or discovered the knowledge in the first place or those whose lives are affected by it in the present — is most hospitable to students' imaginative meaning-making. What makes others' lives meaningful for us is our ability to share imaginatively in their emotions, their fears, hopes, intentions, and so on; to think of them as though they were ours; and to expand our own by thinking of them as possibly like others'. So we connect again with the affective connection.

Humanizing knowledge, then, means teaching it within a context which enables the student to think about it in terms of human needs, hopes, and fears. At the same time this is not at all incompatible with honouring logic and clarity on their own terms. Nor is this a call, as one sees in various teaching-methodology books, for some catchy "hook" for a topic. Rather, it is a call for thinking first about *the human importance of the topic*.

Conclusion

We are still some distance from the typical classroom, but I think these various characteristics of students' imaginative lives provide us with a means of moving there directly now. In the next chapter I will take these characteristics and use them to design planning and teaching techniques.

What has been done in this chapter is to focus on those characteristics of students' intellects that are not very commonly discussed in education. More usually, as I noted earlier, we see such claims as "Research has shown that...", followed by some recommendation for teaching inferred from whatever the research showed. This chapter has provided a more general kind of analysis, which does nevertheless involve a lot of empirical claims about students' thinking and learning. The skeptic might reasonably ask on what basis does it rest, especially as there is very little educational research available on the topic of students' imaginations, and none referred to here. The slightly odd feature of the empirical claims I have made, compared with most research in education, is that they are on the whole uncontentious. The claims are of the kind: it is very common for students during these years to make romantic associations with heroic figures. The examples given are usually so ubiquitous that it would be faintly absurd to run studies to establish that the claim accurately reflects what is the case.

But I should also add that concerning nearly all the characteristics I have discussed there has been done very extensive, large-scale, and hugely expensive empirical research. It has not been carried out by educational researchers, however. It is commonly called "market research", and is funded by those corporations who stand to make huge profits if they can successfully exploit particular characteristics of students' imaginations. If, for example, you want to try your hand at writing a "teen-romance" novel, the publishers who dominate this market can supply you with a set of characteristics which you will need to incorporate in your novel if you hope to engage this age-range. Magazine publishers can do likewise; and the manufacturers of games and toys, and the marketers of movies, T.V. shows, and commercials aimed at this age-range have provided a huge empirical base, from which I have drawn.

Among the characteristics of students' imaginations that one can uncontentiously infer from this data-base are an easy connection with some affective features of a topic; engagement by what is extreme or exotic or which displays something of the limits of a topic; the romantic nature of students and their attraction to the wonderful and awesome; their ready association with the heroic or transcendent; their idealism and easily stimulated sense of injustice that often leads to revolt; their willingness to investigate exhaustively the details of some topic; and an access to knowledge as more direct and spontaneous so long as it is embedded in contexts of human hopes, fears, intentions, and so on. Well, let us see what kind of teaching techniques we can hammer out of this collection of characteristics.

CHAPTER FOUR

Imagination and Teaching

Introduction

The task now is to take the conception of imagination developed in the first two chapters, and the characteristics from the previous chapter, and move in the direction of practical teaching and technique.

What I will do in the first section below is design a framework to help teachers plan lessons or units in such a way that students' imaginations will most likely be engaged in the content to be taught. Most planning frameworks are derived from Tyler's "rationale" (1949) which is in turn, according to Tanner and Tanner (1980), a systematization of principles worked out by John Dewey. These Tyler-derived frameworks tend to follow a basic pattern, as might be expected. Invariably they begin with statements of objectives for the lesson or unit, followed by a selection of content that will meet the objectives, then a choice of methods of instruction best suited to ensure that the particular content serves to meet the objectives, and finally some means of evaluating whether the objectives have indeed been met. While Tyler's work, drawing on Dewey, is clearly hospitable to imaginative activity, the systematizing of his framework over the past forty years or so has fallen increasingly into the hands of people who have aimed at a dessicated sense of efficiency (Callahan, 1962; Kleibard, 1986), and have favoured a more behaviourist approach. Tyler's humane questions thus became reduced to behavioural objectives and crude evaluation procedures. These approaches tend to be in-hospitable to students' imaginative activity. While there is obviously nothing in such objectives-style frameworks that inhibits the imaginative teacher from engaging the imagination of the learner — one might even write it in as an objective — there is equally nothing in such frameworks to encourage imaginative activity. The framework that follows is designed to encourage learning the content and skills of a lesson or unit at least as adequately as objectives-based frameworks, but it is designed to do this by stimulating and developing students' imaginations in the process.

So I will begin by designing a framework that incorporates as many as possible of the characteristics discussed in the previous chapter. Indeed, I think it manages to incorporate them all. (This is not to say that there are not a number of important characteristics that I have missed that could be built into a somewhat different framework.) I will describe how the framework can be used in planning by taking a particular topic and designing a unit plan. As I believe that this framework can be profitably used in planning any topic in any curriculum area, the choice of an example here is more or less arbitrary.

The school curriculum where I live directs students to study the life-cycle of a cold-blooded vertebrate, so I will take for my topic freshwater eels (*Anguillidae* — a word I would have students learn). My purpose here is simply to indicate how the framework can help one to shape the topic to make it imaginatively engaging to students.

After showing how the framework can be used on a particular example — and in the next chapter I will choose examples from several different subject areas to show how it might be used across the curriculum — I will consider a number of less formal and less elaborate ways in which we can convert the characteristics of the previous chapter into principles and techniques for engaging the imagination in learning. I do this to indicate — something which you no doubt hardly need — that one does not have to deploy the whole formal framework in order to draw on the preceding chapter to make teaching more imaginative.

Perhaps it is appropriate to emphasize here that I do not see the framework that follows as some original insight of mine. At one level it is only an attempt to systematize some principles that I see good teachers using all the time, elaborated somewhat by the literature on imagination cited earlier. And particularly with the smaller-scale principles later in this chapter, claims to originality here would be pretentious and silly. Again, they are largely derived from observing the practice of good teachers, reflecting on the character of imaginative activity in typical students, and organizing and systematizing these into the kinds of principles you will see.

A Planning Framework For Imaginative Teaching and Learning

I have laid out the framework (see p. 94) largely as a set of questions, the answers to which should produce a lesson or unit plan. (It is perhaps worth noting, for anyone who has examined or will examine the related framework in *Romantic understanding* [Egan, 1990], that it and the above are different in a number of ways. This is not due to one being an updated model or — in this software age — release 2.0, but rather is intended to indicate that the general principles allow a variety of ways of implementation and that I make no claims that these frameworks are in any sense canonical. I am sure that many readers can adapt this framework and develop significantly different forms that would be improvements. Also, of course, different people have different approaches to teaching, and adaptation of my framework to better suit the individual teacher is to be encouraged.)

Exploration of the Framework by Means of an Example

I will explore how the framework can be used as a planning technique by taking the topic "eels" and working through the framework's stages and sets of questions in turn, and seeing what we come up with.

The first step is to identify within the topic transcendent qualities of the kind discussed in the previous chapter. The question encourages us not just to think about what content about

A PLANNING FRAMEWORK

1. **Identifying transcendent qualities**

    What transcendent human qualities can be seen and felt as central to the topic?
    What affective images do they evoke?

2. **Organizing the content into a narrative structure**

    2.1   **Initial access**

    What content, distinct from students' everyday experience, best embodies the transcendent qualities most central to the topic?
    Does this expose some extreme or limit of reality within the topic?

    2.2   **Structuring the body of the unit or lesson**

    What content best articulates the topic into a clear narrative structure? Briefly sketch the main narrative line.

    2.3   **Humanizing the content**

    How can the content be shown in terms of human hopes, fears, intentions, or other emotions?
    What aspects of the content can best stimulate romance, wonder, and awe?
    What ideals and/or revolts against conventions are evident in the topic?

    2.4   **Pursuing details**

    What content best allows students to pursue some aspect of the topic in exhaustive detail?

3. **Concluding**

    How can one best bring the topic to satisfactory closure, while pointing on to further dimensions or to other topics? How can the students *feel* this satisfaction?

4. **Evaluation**

    How can one know whether the topic has been understood and has engaged and stimulated students' imaginations?

eels we want students to know at the end of the unit, but also to range, as it were, over that content with our affective sensors alive to whatever features stir some emotional response in us, to feel our way into knowledge about eels. This might seem an odd way of beginning, especially to those who have been exposed only to planning frameworks that ask for statements of objectives. But if our aim is to engage students' imaginations, we must first alert and exercise our own, and identify the transcendent qualities in the topic that provide a key to imaginative stimulation.

What might emerge, then, from examining our knowledge of eels with our affective sensors alive? In some people perhaps a rather creepy feeling might be a first affective response, connected no doubt with eels' role in our folklore and subconscious. But our task is to seek out the transcendent in our topic, to learn about eels in such a way that our imaginations are engaged and enlarged, to see what is extraordinary and wonderful about the common fresh-water eel.

No doubt most students will have seen this elongated fish in aquariums or in its natural habitat, and, if not, a visit to an aquarium would obviously be a good idea — though I would delay this until the sense of wonder has been attached to eels. If we range over our knowledge of eels with our affective sensors alert, we might focus on their exotic early life and on the mystery of their procreation. Eels are among the commonest fish in many rivers in Europe and America, yet no-one ever found a milt-bearing or pregnant female, nor found baby eels in any river, nor found eels mating, nor, until relatively recently, could work out whether eels were of different sexes, and, if so, which was which.

Let us take the questions under "Identifying transcendent qualities" one by one. First we are asked what transcendent human qualities can be seen and felt as central to the topic. As with any complex topic, we can identify a large range of such qualities. We could focus on the steady persistence of the eels' strange patterns of migration or their calm evasion of scientific scrutiny even up to the present, refusing to yield their secrets, or their amazing transformations from larvae to elvers (young eels) to mature eels. Alternatively, we can teach what is known about eels by making focal to our unit the transcendent qualities required to have discovered what we do know about them now. In this way we can tie the sense of wonder about the exotic details of the eels' life-cycle to the human curiosity and ingenuity required to discover those details. I will take this perspective here, largely because it is one that could be used commonly with almost any science topic, even if the teacher finds it difficult to identify transcendent human qualities in the topic itself. Some of the transcendent qualities that underlie scientific inquiry, then, become focal: curiosity to know just for knowing's sake, knowledge sought regardless of its utility, and ingenuity and persistence in the search.

What affective images are evoked if we take this persistent, ingenious, and unrelenting search for knowledge as our central transcendent quality? I see the Danish scientist Johannes Schmidt on the decks of various ships criss-crossing the Atlantic from Iceland to the Canary Islands, from North Africa to North America, pulling endless catches aboard and examining their contents in his unrelenting attempt to unravel the mystery of the life-cycle of eels. He began his search in 1904 and continued for twenty years, suspending his voyages reluctantly during the First World War. His unremarked voyages, single-mindedly pursuing knowledge about eels, challenge those of legendary Sinbads or Jasons, and those of Drake, Magellan, and Cook. And what was he doing all those years, braving the Atlantic ocean in all weathers? He was looking for younger and younger eels, elvers, larvae, and tracing them by age in order to locate their breeding grounds.

In the decision to focus on the transcendent qualities bound up in the persistent search for knowledge for its own sake, we have also selected the transcendent quality with which we think students can make strong associations. So let us go on to "Organizing the content into a narrative structure".

First we are asked to consider how best we can provide the students with initial access to the topic through content, distinct from their everyday experience, that best embodies the transcendent qualities we have decided to make central. We might do this by beginning our narrative with the first attempts to answer the mystery of eels' sex-lives. In the ancient world much knowledge had already been accumulated about all kinds of creatures, but eels presented the bizarre mystery of being common and numerous as elvers and adults but unknown as babies; there was never found any milt-bearing or pregnant female — indeed, they were sexually indistinguishable. The Egyptians, Greeks, and Romans considered eel a delicacy, yet despite becoming expert at catching them, they discovered virtually nothing about their life-cycle. Aristotle proposed that the eel was sexless and that its young were created spontaneously out of the mud in river bottoms. Pliny suggested that, when they wanted to procreate, eels rubbed themselves against rocks, and young were formed from the skin thus detached. Other explanations of their birth included that they come from putrefying material in rivers, that they come from the gills of other fishes, that they grew from horses' hairs that dropped into water, or, delightfully, that they were sinful monks whom St. Dunstan in a rage had transformed to do eternal penance (so giving the English cathedral town of Ely its name — the eely place). Linnaeus, the great eighteenth-century biologist, considered the eel to be viviparous, fertilizing its eggs internally and giving birth to its young alive. A problem for this theory arose when it was shown that what had been taken for young eelings in the adult's womb were simply parasitic worms. Through the nineteenth century, intensive research on the biology of eels finally revealed, in 1850, female genitalia, and only in 1874 were tiny testes discovered. But still no-one had any idea of how, when, or where these organs did their reproductive work. No-one had seen an eel's egg or newly-hatched larvae or a ripe female. At the end of the century a tiny transparent, leaf-like fish, quite unlike an eel, was caught in the western Mediterranean. A few earlier similar specimens had been seen and designated a new genus. This particular specimen was reared in captivity, and by a series of amazing transformations grew into an elver and then into an adult eel. (The larvae are called leptocephali — another word for students to learn.) But if eels were so common, why were specimens of eel larvae so very rare? This is where Johannes Schmidt comes into the story, determined to solve the mystery of the eel's life-cycle.

Our initial access, then, is to a consistent, if unsuccessful, quest to understand the life-cycle of the eel. Why bother? What does it matter? The social and political worlds are full of activities for people to occupy their time and energy in immediately fulfilling ways. Why should anyone, let alone dozens of people generation after generation, dedicate their time and energy to find out about eels? Our introduction to the topic is designed to expose a puzzle in such a way that it calls to something within us to answer it. It presents the puzzle in such a way that the response "who cares?" does not arise. While individual students are not going to set out on a persistent quest to resolve the puzzle, they will want to know the resolution of the narrative thus begun. They will very likely understand what it is about eels that engaged Johannes Schmidt in his persistent quest, they are likely ready to travel with him in their imaginations, and they will be ready to think of the possible answers to the puzzle. In laying out our introduction this way we have also provided in our initial access some extreme or limit of reality; the weirdness of eels' life-cycle and the extraordinary puzzles it presented are certainly extreme. (I have said nothing about the method one might use in providing this initial access. Depending on their skills and preferences, teachers might appropriately choose any of a wide variety of methods — audio-visual, inquiry process, straight or illustrated exposition, guided imagery, or whatever.)

We are next asked to select the content that best articulates the topic into a clear narrative line. Sketching this now will be quite easy. We have chosen to take a chronological perspective on the unravelling of the eel's life-cycle, though each new discovery only seems to leave us with further puzzles. And we have set up our narrative so that Schmidt becomes heroic through the ingenuity and persistence he displays in tracing the early life of the eel. It might be useful to set off Schmidt's voyages and discoveries against the social and political background of his time, which forms the focus of most people's attention. While the politicians and soldiers filled centre-stage, wreaking that terrible destruction of the First World War, Schmidt's gradual piecing together of the eel's life-cycle added something perhaps small to our accumulating knowledge. The counterpointing of his slow, persistent inquiry against the cataclysmic events that fill our history texts, might lead to brief meditations on the value of different kinds of activities, and so stimulate some wonder.

Our narrative will follow Schmidt's early explorations in the Mediterranean. He discovered more larvae and found that on average they were larger in size the further east they were caught. So he sailed out into the Atlantic, finding ever smaller larvae drifting in the currents. Schmidt persuaded more than twenty shipowners to collect samples for him, and to chart where each was found. He began to home in on the area where the greatest concentrations of tiny larvae were found, locating their breeding ground between latitudes 20° and 30° North and longitudes 50° and 65° West, in the strange floating weeds that constitute the Sargasso Sea.

We are asked next to consider how the content can be shown in terms of human hopes, fears, intentions, or other emotions. I think we can readily see knowledge about eels in terms of curiosity, frustration, persistence, and ingenuity; we can see occasional pig-headedness, as in the case of Linnaeus's refusal to give up his viviparous theory even in light of the evidence that what he considered eelings were parasitic worms. What aspects of the content can best stimulate romance, wonder, and awe? I think romance can be caught up in the details of Schmidt's voyages and discoveries, in the dedication, the ingenuity, the persistence, the endless miles of the massive Atlantic ocean in search of tiny larvae. Wonder can be stimulated by the strange life-cycle gradually uncovered; the floating larvae carried on currents for months or years and for up to three or four thousand miles, their bizarre transformation from larvae to elvers, their finding — for thousands of years that we know of — the same rivers of Europe and America, their peculiar sexual progress from neuter, to precocious feminization, to hermaphrodite, before settling for male or female conditions, their unfailing migration back to the sea after about ten years in their freshwater home rivers. Awe might be stimulated by just considering the purpose of all this remarkable complexity in eels' life-cycle. Why? As for ideals and revolt, one could contrast the scientific virtues of persistence and ingenuity, and the permanence of its discoveries, with conventional engagements in the immediate and in knowledge of practical utility. The dedication to solving the mysteries of eels' life-cycles becomes comprehensible within the context of the narrative we have set up, and ideally it will help students both to appreciate and to partake in the scientific enterprise that Schmidt has epitomized here.

This topic provides a wealth of details that might be fairly exhaustively pursued: charting the changes from larvae to elvers; the foods of eels at various stages of life; Schmidt's voyages; the variety of forms of larvae, from threadlike to saucerlike forms, and the adult forms they grow into; the families of eels; the Sargasso Sea; and so on.

We are next asked how to bring this topic to satisfactory closure. One might provide in conclusion a different narrative, this time bringing together the sequential outline of the eel's life-cycle, from the Sargasso Sea to American and European rivers, and back again. In this telling we might highlight those aspects of their life-cycle that are still not known or understood. We still lack, for example, a clear image of how male and female eels reproduce in the Sargasso Sea. We do not know how many of, or even whether, the European eels who set off on their long migration back to the Sargasso Sea ever make it. We do not know the mechanisms that trigger and guide their migrations; we might connect this with other creatures with exotic migration patterns — salmon, birds, butterflies, etc.

We might employ various methods to evaluate a unit such as this. We will want to ensure that students have learned in detail about eels and their life-cycle, and also that they know which features of eels' lives remain mysterious. We can use traditional forms of evaluation to inform us about students' knowledge — using tests, examining their written work, grading projects, and so on.

Because we have been trying to engage students' imaginations with eels, we will also want to evaluate how successful we have been in this regard. Obviously we do not have well-tried and tested evaluation procedures that will give us precise readings of imaginative engagement, and probably never will have. But we might experiment with plausible ways of getting some kind of reading. We might begin, simply, with teachers' observation. It is usually fairly clear whether or not students are imaginatively engaged in a topic; the degree of their enthusiasm, the way it invades their intellectual activity in general, their pursuit of aspects of it well beyond what is required, their questioning and searching out additional sources of information, their desire simply to talk about it, are all indicators of some degree of imaginative engagement. Students' written work, or other forms in which they present what they have learned to the teacher or to the class as a whole, can yield evidence of imaginative engagement; going beyond what is required, especially when the direction has been determined perhaps by the student's idiosyncratic interests, or taking great care in, for example, drawing different forms of larvae or species of eel, or evidence of knowledge that has been culled from diverse sources not readily available, or evidence of a kind of obsessive interest in some feature of eels' lives, would all provide some indication of imaginative engagement. Some of the above characteristics of students' work could, of course, be due to other factors, like desire for a high grade or compulsion. But it is an unusually unobservant teacher who cannot tell the difference. These points echo, in brief, ideas that are elaborated and developed in Eisner's "connoisseurship" model of evaluation (Eisner, 1985).

This is an area in which one might encourage students' self-evaluation. Ask them to reflect on how far they felt they had been imaginatively engaged in the topic, what features of it engaged them most, what had they most enjoyed learning about, and so on. This might also become a useful small-group activity, in which individual interests might incidentally be communicated to the group.

A part of the attempt to evaluate a unit such as this must involve trying to discover how far students grasp the underlying scientific virtue of pursuing knowledge purely for its own sake, and recognizing persistence and ingenuity as appropriately serving this pursuit. Also we will want to evaluate how far students associate with these transcendent human qualities. We can try to get some reading of these from students' work, from their classroom behaviour, and from effects on what they more readily turn their minds to in leisure time. The sensitive teacher will no doubt be able to get an adequate reading on their success, even though it will not be in terms of some precise score. (We decide what it is educationally valuable to do on grounds other than what we can evaluate precisely.)

There has been a considerable development in recent years of what are generally called "qualitative evaluation" procedures. Many of these would be useful here. A clear introduction and discussion of some of these procedures is available in Schubert (1986), and more elaboration and detail is available in Guba and Lincoln (1981) and in Patton (1990).

Perhaps I might conclude this example by making what may seem the obvious point that the more one knows about a topic the easier it is to find transcendent qualities within it and to make it imaginatively engaging to others. There are, of course, experts who seem unable to make their area of expertise interesting to others, but those individuals would not be helped by knowing less. Lest it should be thought that enormous amounts of knowledge are thus required before this framework can be used at all, I should first confess that my total knowledge of eels comes from a few pages of Graham Swift's novel *Waterland* (1983), which I have drawn on liberally and gratefully, and about half an hour with an encyclopaedia. And, second, even this small amount of reading is not necessary to re-see and reorganize whatever knowledge one has of a topic in order to make it more imaginatively engaging for others. The framework above is designed to provide some help in this process, and I hope it does.

Less Formal Implementations: Fragmenting the Framework

A teacher, persuaded that the above framework might be worth trying, might first follow it step by step answering the questions as I have done above. No doubt this would be done in an abbreviated note-form rather than in the lengthy discursive form I have used for purposes of illustration. Similarly, pre-service teachers might want to practice organizing a topic in this format as well as in more conventional ways, seeing which leads to more successful teaching for them. If it works well, no doubt teachers might try it again on another unit or on a single lesson. While it may appear a bit cumbersome initially, I suspect that with a little practice the time required to deal with most of the questions will reduce significantly, allowing most time to be spent on the central structuring of the content (in section 2.2 of the framework). Certainly, this reflects the experience of most of the teachers I have worked with.

But many teachers have planning procedures or patterns that work well for them, and they will not want to adopt a whole new and elaborate framework — unless, that is, it contains many elements they already use and others that seem attractive, or unless initial experiences trying it are successful beyond expectations. But for many teachers, one or more of the parts of the framework might seem attractive, and they may wish to assimilate it or them into their usual planning procedures. In this section I will discuss briefly how this might be done. In the following section I will discuss an alternative that would likely have a similar result. That is, instead of dealing with the framework at all, we could go back to the characteristics of the previous chapter and convert each of them into a principle of learning that teachers could draw on at any time. The first alternative, "fragmenting the framework", I will deal with briefly. The second alternative can also be dealt with quite briefly after the earlier discussion, but I will elaborate it a little with examples.

So, teachers can obviously take whichever parts of the framework they might find useful and ignore the rest, fitting whatever they choose into their own usual planning procedures, however formal or informal they may be. Perhaps just the first step of the framework suggests something novel and useful to some teachers. The notion of looking for transcendent qualities, affective images, and engaging students' imaginative associations with such qualities might seem worthwhile. This could even be incorporated into an objectives-based planning framework, perhaps influencing the selection of content. It could serve as an additional consideration drawing attention to dimensions of a topic that might otherwise be neglected. In most planning schemes we are not encouraged to look for this dimension of human experience in the content we present to students. So incorporating just this item might enlarge and enrich what is routinely considered.

Teachers might narrow even further what they take from the framework. Some might find that the notion of seeking an affective image that is evoked when they reflect on the human significance of the topic would make a useful addition to their planning. Quite commonly such images can then be introduced to students as ways of evoking for them in turn something of the affective dimension of the topic, whatever the subject area. The capacity to evoke such images seems to be one that is greatly enhanced and facilitated by practice. Teachers might find that they can also engage the students in evoking such images as well.

If one were to take only item 2.1 from the framework, concerning initial access, it could provide an alternative approach to that which is usually recommended for beginning a unit or lesson. The engaging power of what is most distinct from students' present knowledge and experience, especially where it involves the limits and extremes of people's lives or of the physical world, might be drawn on occasionally. Thus, rather than seeking to begin with the familiar, now and then teachers might be persuaded to try this "opposite". It is not really an opposite, as I have suggested earlier, because each ideally feeds the other. But it is apparently a procedure directly opposed to what is the prevailing wisdom about how to engage students' interest in a topic. Particularly if attention is given to seeking content that embodies transcendent human qualities, this alternative might prove surprisingly effective. A research study I am currently conducting involves asking adults what they recall of the history they were taught at school. Nearly all the subjects report finding Social Studies interesting and still memorable when it began to introduce topics dealing with strange and unfamiliar material.

The idea of looking for a story-like narrative structure when organizing the content of a lesson or unit could also be adapted to an objectives-based scheme. The effect would be to insert an additional consideration when selecting content. The addition would involve selecting content that brings out an affective dimension. The narrative line, or story-plotting, works by identifying within the topic a pattern that makes sense not just logically but also emotionally. That is, the topic moves forward in a way that makes emotional sense as well as logical sense. The connection between the lessons in the unit, or between different sub-topics, is thus not simply a logical one. It will, of course, have a logical component, but the addition to structuring content contributed by item 2.2 of the framework is the location of affective connections.

I realize that this is not an easy principle to grasp, or perhaps I realize simply that I am unable to articulate it clearly. In mitigation, I suspect some of the difficulty — if indeed it exists — is due in part to the ways we have tended to separate the logical structuring of content from anything that could be considered emotional. Think of a Shakespeare play for a moment. The connection between any two scenes has to make logical sense but commonly the main connection is one that makes sense because of the pattern of emotions the play has set up. In *Hamlet* the scene where Hamlet jokingly tells the King where dead Polonius lies "at supper...Not where he eats, but where he is eaten" precedes the scene in which Fortinbras and his army pass through Denmark on their way to war against Poland. The connection between the two scenes makes sense to us, not by any simple logical causality, but rather by an affective causality which we can follow because we see the two scenes in terms of Hamlet's confused emotions.

The other component that can be added by incorporating item 2.2 into a planning scheme is the setting up of a tension between binary opposites at the beginning of the narrative structuring of a lesson or unit. This is an element found in most stories. Such binary opposites need not be entirely dominant but they can help to provide an affective tension to a unit or lesson that can make it much more meaningful and engaging to students.

Item 2.3 of the framework concerns humanizing the content to be taught. This by itself is hardly an original notion. It was given an extensive modern formulation by John Dewey. But teachers could pull out of the framework the idea that one should always pause to consider the content of a lesson or unit as in some way a product of, a cause of, or related to, human hopes, fears, intentions, and so on. So instead of teaching polynomials in mathematics as just a set of manipulations and algorithms to be learned, one will pause and search either for the human emotions involved in the initial invention of this branch of mathematics — who? why? what kind of people? what was the story involved? — or for how their use affects people's lives in the present — what human use is this branch of mathematics put to? While this way of thinking about content, despite John Dewey's work, is still not a normal part of teacher-preparation programmes, a bit of practice makes it seem, as it should, quite natural and straightforward. After all, it is through human lives at one time or another that all the content we teach came to be and has meaning.

In some curriculum areas, the "humanizing" of the content will seem rather easier than in others. In history and literature the centrality of people's lives, and their emotions and intentions, make such subjects more readily accessible to this treatment. But mathematics and science are no less products of human emotions and intentions, and grasping those can be the surest way to grasping the meaning of the mathematics and science. With textbooks that brought out the human aspects of these subjects, the work of teachers and students would be much easier.

Perhaps some teachers think they already attend to many of the above issues, though possibly using different terms for them, but the obsessive collecting and hobbies that students engage in during these years may be suggestive of something they have not consciously exploited before. Everyone recognizes that students can become enthusiastic in pursuing something in detail, but perhaps the connection with an exhaustible aspect of a topic in the sense developed above might persuade some teachers to incorporate item 2.4 of the framework into their planning. The central point is to encourage students to explore in detail something that they can, if not exhaust, at least discover the limits of, and that allows them some sense of making appreciable progress towards exhausting it. An important part of this item would be to enable and encourage the students to organize, lay out, and/or display the detailed knowledge they are accumulating as though it were a "collection".

The final two items will probably already be a part of any planning procedure, however formally or informally they are carried out. The possible further dimension offered by item 3 of the framework is concerned with what we have looked at with regard to item 2.2 — the narrative organization. Concluding in the manner recommended in this framework is distinguished by its relationship to the story-structuring. Similarly, item 4 only becomes distinctive if one has already incorporated significant features of the framework into one's teaching. One would obviously not bother to evaluate success in stimulating students' imaginations in the way this framework suggests if that was not among one's specific objectives.

From Characteristics to Principles of Learning

An alternative procedure, one that allows teachers to draw on particular ideas incorporated in the framework without using the whole scheme, is to move more directly from the characteristics described in the previous chapter to a set of principles of learning. We are accustomed to think of "principles of learning" more in terms of what are commonly called "cognitive" features of students' minds, whereas here I will be trying to derive some principles from discussions of imagination and "affective" features of students' minds. I put it in this odd way because I think such distinctions as "cognitive" and "affective" more often are misleading than helpful in education. The focus on "affective" features and on imagination here and in the framework is not, I hope obviously, to suggest in any way that the intellectual activities engaged in by the students are any the less "cognitive". My emphasis on the "affective" is not at all to displace the "cognitive", but is intended rather to assert a necessary and neglected component of rational, cognitive activity. "Rationality" or "cognitive activity" that lacks imaginative and affective components is dessicated and inadequate. So the principles to be discussed here are important features of adequate intellectual functioning which have too commonly been ignored in educational discourse.

The task, then, is to show how one can take the characteristics of the previous chapter and convert them to principles of learning that teachers can draw on in practice. There is nothing particularly problematic about this. No doubt, teachers reading the previous chapter, if they find some characteristic they are not already familiar with, would be able to adapt them to principles themselves and in their own way, but I will briefly indicate some possible ways of doing this.

The subheadings of the previous chapter suggest a set of characteristics of students' imaginative lives. Let us, then, take in turn "affective connections", "extremes and limits of reality", "romance, wonder and awe", "associating with the heroic", "revolt and idealism", "matters of detail", and "humanizing knowledge". Each of these can become a principle that can be drawn on to guide teaching. Together they can serve as a kind of tool-kit of principles that can supplement those learned in pre-service programmes, in workshops, and in discussions with other teachers.

So, the observations in "the affective connection" about narrative structuring or story shaping can become a particular principle that can be drawn on wherever teachers find it appropriate. With some practice it should prove possible for teachers to adopt and adapt this principle easily and flexibly. Either in planning or in the middle of teaching a topic, a teacher might draw on the principle of narrative structuring to create a tension between binary opposites located in the topic, or by generating an unresolved expectation. At a more superficial level, the principle can be employed by introducing some anecdote that can enliven and add meaning to a topic, and so engage students' interest. The use of anecdotes as a principle derived from the characterization of "the affective connection" directs us to look for those that show up some of the most important ideas involved in the topic — as distinct from anecdotes that might be engaging for the moment but only of peripheral interest to the topic as a whole. That is, even though the use of anecdotes may be more superficial than structuring the whole unit as a coherent narrative, their use according to this principle requires that we get at what is affectively central to our topic.

For example, in the middle of a routine lesson on rock formations the teacher might take a break and tell the story of "the Great Devonian controversy" (see Gould, 1988), in which the characters involved in discovering the basis for our modern understanding of rock formations dramatically confronted each other with competing theories. Or, searching for a binary structure to hold the detailed knowledge and provide a narrative line one might choose ice and fire; the former slow and strong, the latter fast and fierce. One could tell much of the story of rock formation in terms of their alternating domination.

Using students' ready engagement with the extremes and limits of reality provides another tool for expanding imaginative grasp on a topic. While this may seem like mere sensationalism, if it is remembered rather as a setting of an important boundary context for the topic at hand, it can serve as a far from trivial contributor to understanding. The teacher who recognizes the value of this context-establishing has available a principle that can be deployed to enrich any topic taught. Such a teacher will remain alert not just to the particular content that constitutes the topic, but also to the exotic extremes within which it exists and which exist within it. The teacher can, as it were, zoom in or out to quite different levels of generality in the content, helping to embed it more clearly by thinking of it within strange but real extremes and limits.

Students learning decimals and fractions might be given a brief excursion into other counting systems. They could be shown how the ancient Babylonians counted up to, say, thirteen, as compared with the Egyptians of the classical period and the Romans or the Mayans, and then how computers count up to thirteen using binary code. They might then be asked to extend those systems up to twenty. Most students would enjoy the puzzle aspect of this, but would also get an interesting sense of how we indicate numbers. They might then be asked how in these systems fractions, or parts of numbers, might be indicated. This exercise, fun in itself, provides some context for appreciating something of the ingenuity of the Arabic system we use.

For very many topics the provision of a means for collecting "records" or extreme and weird features would enable students themselves to seek out limits and provide a context as they go along. If studying trees, they might discover which is the oldest known tree, the tallest, the smallest, the one with the shortest life span, the fastest growing, the kind that produces the most seeds (how many?), and so on.

Romance, wonder, and awe provide a multi-dimensional principle to enhance learning of any topic. If teachers are familiar with these characteristics of students' imaginative lives, and become adept at identifying romance, wonder, and awe in any topic they teach, they have available a means of heightening its significance and enlarging its meaning. The teacher who can develop the capacity to "heroize" aspects of reality, whether styrofoam cups, mathematical algorithms, or historical movements, can draw flexibly and frequently on this capacity to stimulate romance, wonder, and awe in students. Frequent uses of this principle, quite briefly perhaps and low-key, can open students' minds like spring-woken trees. After the previous discussion I suspect examples of this principle at work are superfluous.

It is evident that the characteristic of associating with the heroic converts into a principle closely related to the above. The point to emphasize here is that the association is to be made with a transcendent human quality. To utilize this principle, teachers must develop skill and flexibility in searching and identifying a range of such qualities in whatever is the topic to be taught.

If our subject is the earthworm, then we might employ this principle by heroizing the fertility and abundance of this seemingly defenceless and simple animal. One might pause from the more routine instruction to consider the sheer quantity of earthworms within a mile of the school. The easy relationship of this principle with that deriving from romance, wonder, and awe may be seen in of the "heroized" worm, and can lead to learning a series of wonders that emerge from considering various of its 1,800 species. This in turn can be connected with extremes and limits by encouraging students to find out about some of the strangest earthworms, such as the Australian species that grows to over three metres long, those that climb trees, and so on.

The characteristics of revolt and idealism can similarly become a principle to be added to the teacher's pedagogical tool-kit. For students this is a period when ideals are commonly formed, and their readiness to revolt or protest against whatever stands in the way of realizing those ideals is one of the ways that students' imaginative lives project into and grasp the world and experience. If the teacher is sensitive to the readiness whereby students associate with revolt against forces that threaten ideals, then this imaginative capacity can both be engaged by a topic and enhanced in being exercised. Many topics in science or history or other subjects will provide ways of showing the subject matter in such terms.

Nearly all science topics, for example, can be shown as involving a revolt against conventional ideas. The ideal of establishing what is the case has been constantly fought against by those who believe on improper grounds that they already know what the case is. This could be a structuring theme for everything from basic cosmology to the study of light, gases, and on and on. Similarly in history, the association with the ideals of those who wished to abolish slavery, for example, or who wished for a more humane factory system, can engage the students, and their revolt against those who tried to perpetuate those systems can encourage imaginative engagement with the topic. Obviously the teacher needs to be cautious in employing this principle, ensuring that it does not become merely an easy tool of ideologizing or of self-congratulation or of glorifying winners.

The interest in detail leads to a principle that is an easy one to bear in mind. As a teacher working with some of these ideas wrote a few days ago: "I've noticed how some kids just let details go in one ear or eye and out the other. Yet those same kids, if it is something they are truly interested in and have freely chosen, will collect information for months and months and have every little bit of it emblazoned in their memories. I would guess that in broad topics there would be some specific area that each student would be interested in collecting details about, and especially if they could organize it as though it were a 'collection'" (Susan Zuckerman, 1990).

What I have tried to suggest above are some of the principles that can help trigger students' interest in particular details, rather than let them go in one ear or eye and out the other. Further examples are probably unnecessary here, but the point about the exhaustibility, or the possibility of getting an adequate sense of the scale of something, is perhaps worth mentioning again. If teachers bear this principle in mind, it will encourage occasionally breaking the routine pattern of instruction to allow for such detailed work. Obviously this is hardly a novel recommendation. Common "project-work" can provide one means of utilizing this principle effectively.

Once "humanizing knowledge" is converted to a principle teachers carry around, it can serve as an explicit pedagogical reminder that a topic might be brought to imaginative life for students more readily if it is seen through the emotions of the people who are involved with it. This principle encourages us constantly to think of any topic not only in terms of its content and organization but to attend to it with our affective sensors alert. We want to locate those areas that can help to vivify the content by bringing out the hopes, fears, and purposes of people within it. Applying this principle to our early study of genetics would encourage us to see the knowledge about genetics not as some finished, neatly organized set of facts to be learned, but as growing through the hopes and ambitions and patience and ingenuity of the people who generated it. An understanding of the detailed knowledge is the aim in both cases. By "humanizing" the knowledge we make it more meaningful and imaginatively engaging for students.

Conclusion

As I noted in the book's introduction, I have looked at this framework and these principles of learning very much from the teacher's point of view. In saying, for example, that teachers must be alert to bringing out whatever is heroic in a topic, or must search for the human emotions and make those clear to the students, I do not wish to suggest that students should be expected to be merely passive recipients of this teacherly activity: as though they are to sit like automata waiting for teachers to evoke and stimulate them to imaginative life. My whole argument is that students are typically imaginatively alive, frequently more imaginatively alive than adults, but that we have allowed curricula and instruction aimed at producing measurable learning to suppress or depress that imaginative activity, at least as far as the content of the curriculum is concerned. Now obviously this overstates the case, and that "we" does not apply to the many energetic teachers who routinely engage students' imaginations with mathematics, literature, and other subjects. But somehow the influence of the factory model on schools, so pervasive through this century, has emphasized measurable "products" over meaning, understanding, emotional significance, and, generally, imagination.

So my talking here of the teacher's role in stimulating students is in part due only to my assuming that it is too obvious to need reiteration that this role may often need interpreting as the teacher being alert to students' spontaneously making romantic associations, or humanizing knowledge, or "heroizing" some feature of a topic. In such cases the teacher can encourage, help elaborate, help engage other students, and so on.

A point that can bear much emphasis is that the above framework and principles are not of a kind that lend themselves to being mechanically applied. No doubt someone could, as it were, fill in the blanks by answering the framework's questions in a routine and dull way. But the call on teachers to construct affective images requires primarily that they vivify their own *feelings* with regard to the subject matter. This framework cannot be adequately used if planning is seen solely as a conceptual task; it has to be *also* an affective task. No teacher can reasonably expect to be able to implement, for example, the principle about "heroizing" content unless he or she can, as it were, turn that perspective on the content and *feel* its heroism. Heroizing aspects of reality requires teachers to develop this capacity in themselves, until they can take such a "romantic" perspective readily on any subject matter. So putting these principles into one's pedagogical tool-kit is not simply a matter of memorizing the list for ready reference. I hope their implementation will indeed become easy and routine. Getting them into one's tool-kit, however, especially for teachers and student-teachers who may find this range of skills unfamiliar and underdeveloped in their own professional-development programmes, will require some practice. If they are not capacities already a part of teachers' intellectual lives, they will need to become so.

Because of the educational importance of imagination, it seems to me that learning how to engage and stimulate students' imaginations should have a central place in teacher-preparation programmes. Where there is an emphasis on imagination it is usually the result of particular individuals' energy. What seems commonly the overriding emphasis on teaching a variety of important management skills tends to squeeze concern with imagination to the margins of most professional-development programmes. This seems yet another case of putting our mechanical carts before our organic horses. Surely it is important to institutionalize the educational priority of equipping pre-service teachers with the capacities to readily engage students' imaginations, while preserving, as a subsidiary but still necessary set of skills, the management techniques that are required to make the former possible.

CHAPTER FIVE

Image and Concept

This very brief chapter was to have been the final point of my conclusion to the previous chapter, but it is so central to my argument for giving more attention to stimulating students' imaginations that I wanted to give it special emphasis.

In the framework of the previous chapter I include the question about what affective images are evoked by the topic to be taught. This is, at least in my experience of pre-service professional-development programmes, an unusual question. Much more commonly, student-teachers might be asked to focus clearly on the concepts or the content they wish to communicate. But in oral cultures, in literature, in film and T.V., it has always been recognized that important meaning can be very effectively communicated by embedding it in affective images. If we want understanding — a grasp both of the knowledge and its significance — to be conveyed to the mind of our hearer, reader, or watcher, then the message can most effectively be carried by an affective image. The image does not displace anything, it carries the concept from mind to mind; if the concept is what we want carried, the image can be an efficient vehicle. Image and concept are not at war in our minds; they properly complement each other.

Now, clearly, this is dangerous ground. Our cultural history can be told in significant part as a battle for dominance between concept and image, between reason and rhetoric, between logic and emotion, and on and on through the many ways we have bifurcated features of our thinking. Plato's implacable opposition to the rhetoricians and his immense influence on educational thinking down to our own day, means that no-one can cheerfully pop up and recommend more attention to imagination without running into buffeting rumbles of this long battle. It requires considerable innocence of our intellectual history and our present forms of thought to think such recommendations can be casually implemented. The institutions in which teachers are prepared have incorporated, in ways that are clearly unconscious to many of those who operate within them, a range of presuppositions that see the concept and the image as in conflict for control of the mind, and that are committed to the priority of the concept over the image. I am not arguing for the reverse. I am arguing that the opposition is a false one; that a conception of rationality that does not see imagination as its "inscape" is sterile, and so development of the imagination is crucial to the development of rationality.

So, even though I explicitly touch on the evoking of affective images only once in the previous chapter, my general argument about the educational value of imagination implies an extended recommendation to teachers to be more attentive to images, and to the metaphors that they move on. We have given pride of place to the disembedded concept in education, and seem largely to have forgotten what all the most powerful communicative media in our cultural history make plain to us, that the affective image is crucial in communicating meaning and significance.

Affective images, as discussed in Chapter One, are not necessary to all imaginative activity. Nor are all quasi-pictorial images affective. Students engaged in Shepard's experiments, rotating images of geometrical shapes, obviously are not likely to be emotionally involved. But it is clear that one significant and common kind of imaginative activity is thinking, and feeling, with quasi-pictorial images. It is this capacity that seems to have received too little systematic attention, and encouragement, in education.

In the example used earlier I have tried to capture something of the persistence and ingenuity that have been required to discover what we know about eels through the image of Johannes Schmidt on the deck of one of his rusting hulks trawling the Atlantic for larvae. One could embellish this image very simply — see the various ships tossed in storms, becalmed in tropics, facing the weedy mystery of the Sargasso Sea. In the first example of the next chapter I will try to get at the romance of the geometrical theorem about congruent alternate interior angles formed by a transversal across parallel lines through the image of Eratosthenes in an Egyptian courtyard measuring the shadow of an upright piece of wood. Any topic we have to deal with is potentially rich with vivid images. We are so conditioned to focus on concepts that we commonly do not even notice or attend to the images that throng our minds when we think about curriculum content.

If we study the ancient Egyptians or the Greeks or medieval cathedrals or castles, we commonly use books with pictures. These can, of course, help students to form images but, perhaps paradoxically, pictures often do little to stimulate mental images. (It takes considerable art to achieve this — such as David Macauley [1973, 1975, 1977] achieves in his books on castles, cathedrals, pyramids, etc. Though it should be added, a significant part of his success is due to embedding the illustrations in vivid narratives.) Those images that have most power for us are those we generate ourselves from words. Anyone who has seen the film of a book they have loved will recognize my point here. The film's pictures can rarely capture the emotional force of the mental images we formed while reading. And this is why film can so rarely evoke and stimulate our imaginative responses with anything like the force of literature. This is to emphasize that I am not calling for more visual illustration of topics, but rather for the teacher to be hospitable to the mental images that any topic evokes and to hunt among them for those with most vivid power to carry the content most richly to students' minds. And to use these often. This doesn't require enormous effort and production. Occasional anecdotal interludes can achieve this kind of effect quite easily.

If we study earthworms, we will do well to feel ourselves slither and push, tentatively explore a direction looking for softer passages through the soil, contracting and expanding our rippling muscles in the direction of scents, moisture, grubs. That is, as we learn about the anatomy of an earthworm we have to feel our way into that anatomy, to feel how the world would feel and taste and smell with that anatomy. If we study trees, we similarly evoke images and sensations, waking and opening to the spring sun, the throbbing sap, the ecstacy of flower and fruit, the slowing cold and curling back into our sleeping barky shell for winter. If we study auto-mechanics or dressmaking, we could become the tools and the fabrics moving together, or sense the parts working into a unit, the power and the ingenuity and the beauty. It sounds romantic; it is romantic. But without the sense of romance that vivid images can convey, the content remains dull, dry, and meaningless.

That is, the image can carry the imagination to inhabit in some sense the object of our study and inquiry. By such means mathematics and ecology, science and history, auto-mechanics and dressmaking are not exterior things that we learn facts about but become a part of us; we are mathematical, scientific, historical, manufacturing people — our culture is our nature.

CHAPTER SIX

Some Further Examples

Introduction

In this chapter I will give four further examples of topics in different curriculum areas planned according to the framework. While I think it is important to try to move from the more abstract realm of principles in the direction of techniques, there is always the danger that technique will become disconnected from principle. So I want to emphasize again that the framework is just one example of the principles about engaging students' imagination, and will work only to the degree that its use exemplifies them. The focus of this book is the principles underpinning imagination in teaching and learning; the framework and examples are intended only to provide a more concrete articulation of them. Ideally, of course, it is by internalizing the principles into thinking and practice that teachers can best use them in their own ways. The framework is intended as a kind of crutch which might well be discarded once teachers have internalized the principles in ways that suit their personal style and practice.

I will not deal with the variety of methods teachers might use in presenting the content — whether inquiry processes here or cooperative learning there, or whatever methods might be deployed. There are many books on such topics and a wealth of illustrative literature. Nor will I try to give a detailed account of the content. In brief, what I want to provide here is not a unit on government drawn up in such detail that a teacher could walk into class with it next Monday and start teaching. Rather I want to provide a demonstration of the framework in sufficient detail that a teacher can take it and apply it to other topics — adding it, as it were, to his or her pedagogical tool-kit. So, to draw on the well-known Chinese proverb, I am not trying to provide a fish here, but teach a method of fishing.

Mathematics

If I flick open one of my children's mathematics books, and turn back a page to the beginning of a section, I am faced with geometry and a theorem: "Parallel lines cut by a transversal form congruent alternate interior angles." How can the framework help in organizing this topic so that it will be imaginatively engaging to students? Let's lay it out category by category and see what we get.

Identifying Transcendent Qualities

The historical development of geometry advanced far, very early. It showed the practical side of energetic inquiring minds at work. Geometry gave a grasp over an aspect of the world which was at one level purely theoretical but had, at another, remarkable practical consequences. Geometry worked like magic: from a small data base and a handful of theorems one could work out or discover some amazing facts about the world. We will want to catch at this sense of the magic, or at least the wonderful, that is a part of geometry. The transcendent quality of practical ingenuity might provide an affective backbone to our lesson or unit. We will try to forge an association between the students and this quality.

Is there an image than can catch at this affective quality? What in the world connected with congruent alternate interior angles can evoke the sense of practical ingenuity? I see the venerable director of the library at Alexandria very carefully erecting a rod in a courtyard, ensuring that it is exactly vertical, and then measuring the angle of the shadow cast by the sun. What he is doing, with his simple tools, is calculating the circumference of the earth.

Organizing the Content into a Narrative Structure

Initial access to the topic might usefully be provided in this case through the image we formed. In part anticipating the requirement that we "humanize" the content, we can begin by introducing the students to the formidable polymath, Eratosthenes of Cyrene (c. 275 - 194 B.C.). He was one of those omnivorous inquirers with a distinct practical bent, in the style of Leonardo da Vinci. He did significant work in astronomy, history, literary criticism (including a twelve-volume work, *On Ancient Comedy*), philosophy, poetry, and mathematics. He also devised a calendar, with leap years. He calculated the distances of the moon and the sun from the earth, though not as accurately as his calculation of the earth's circumference. In old age he became blind and, so the story goes, voluntarily starved himself to death. Such an introduction also can catch at some extremes of reality and experience.

We will, then, structure the body of this short unit by beginning with Eratosthenes' method of calculating the circumference of the earth, seeing the theorem ingeniously applied to a practical problem. We will then move on to other cases of the utility of the theorem, and then consider briefly the kinds of disembedded examples that constitute the exclusive concern of most current textbooks. As a part of this move from historical examples to the disembedded theorem, I would include some procedure for visualizing the relationship of such angles — something that no longer requires tricky moving models now that one can simulate such models on a computer. One would, that is, set up a simple model of a parallelogram with a transverse line such that students could change the shape of the parallelogram and see the alternate interior angles changing congruently.

How did Eratosthenes use the theorem to calculate the earth's circumference using a vertical rod in Alexandria? Five hundred miles to the south of Alexandria, on what we call the Tropic of Cancer, was the town of Syene, on the site of present-day Aswan. (This calculation works out more neatly in miles than in kilometres.) Eratosthenes knew that at noon on the summer solstice in Syene a vertical rod cast no shadow. He also knew that the sun was very distant from the earth and that its rays could be considered as striking different places on the earth in parallel. So to our image. Around 200 B.C. Eratosthenes mounted a vertical rod in Alexandria and at noon on the summer solstice he measured the angle its shadow cast. From that measure he calculated with remarkable accuracy, by means of our theorem, the circumference of the earth. How?

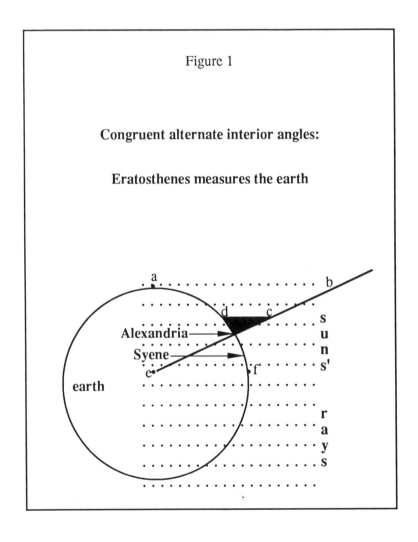

Figure 1

Congruent alternate interior angles:

Eratosthenes measures the earth

Consider the diagram in Figure 1. From the theorem Eratosthenes (with whose name students should obviously become familiar and they should be able to pronounce it accurately) knew that <ABE and <BEF in the above diagram are congruent alternate interior angles — i.e., whatever <ABE is, <BEF will be the same. By holding a pole upright in Alexandria he held it along the line EB. The top of the pole forms <ECD, which is also congruent with <ABE and <BEF. Eratosthenes' careful measurement of the angle of the shadow at noon — <ECD — yielded 7° 12'. That meant that <BEF must also be 7° 12'. 7° 12' is about 1/50 of the 360° of a full circle, and so the distance from Alexandria to Syene was 1/50 of the circumference of the earth. 50 x 500 = 25,000, so the circumference of the earth must be about 25,000 miles — which it is.

While it is easier to work out with cities on or within the tropics, one can still use this method with any two cities distant from each other that are on much the same longitude. Teachers in, say, Toronto and Miami, or Calgary and Phoenix, or Melbourne and Cooktown, could arrange to measure the angle cast by the sun at noon on particular days, compare figures and, with slight modification, use Eratosthenes' method to calculate the earth's circumference. This might make a "re-embedding" activity that could conclude the narrative of the unit.

Humanizing the content should be relatively easy by extending the association with Eratosthenes' practical ingenuity. He exemplifies a magus-like cleverness. He did not need to travel around the world, measuring distance in the conventional ways. Using the ingenious techniques of geometry — a kind of magic too casually taken for granted — he was able to calculate the earth's circumference to within a few miles, at a time when most of its inhabitants had no idea even that it was round. We would do well to work at bringing to the fore the awe, wonder, and romance of geometry, rather than treating it as a set of routine, taken-for-granted techniques to be learnt. By associating with Eratosthenes', and others', ingenuity in calculating distances to the moon and sun, and the earth's circumference, by ingeniously extending from what was already known, one can help students become engaged by what is remarkable and wonderful about geometry. Geometry, and mathematics in general, can thus be seen, not just as an endless set of algorithms and theorems, but as a romantic adventure.

The convention that we can represent Eratosthenes revolting against is that which accepts the unknown as unknowable, which feels powerless in the face of whatever is beyond the boundary of established norms and routines. The ideal he represents is the determined use of practical ingenuity to achieve what to the conventional mind is impossible. Some elementary geometry was deployed to perform the remarkable feat of calculating the earth's circumference.

Concluding

Useful details that might elaborate this topic and its association with practical ingenuity could include a study of what is known of Eratosthenes' life and his other achievements; the lives and practical ingenuity of other Greek geometers; what is known of the library at Alexandria; other practical uses for the theorem; and so on.

Evaluation

One can use traditional forms of evaluation to discover whether students understand the geometrical principle and can apply it to new cases. Given our intention, we will also want to look for evidence that students have associated in some degree with the quality of practical ingenuity which Eratosthenes has exemplified for us. A difficulty with looking for precise measures of such qualities is that they may take different forms in each individual's behaviour. But the observant teacher would be able to use practical ingenuity to measure whether or not, or the degree to which, students find the discovery of congruence in alternate interior angles imaginatively engaging. At the simplest level, their enthusiasm would provide an index, as would their interest in learning about some mathematicians and geometers contemporary with Eratosthenes, such as Archimedes, Nicomedes, and others. I suspect that the results of the traditional evaluation procedures might also give some insight into students' association with practical ingenuity, as I would anticipate much better results from traditional tests after such a method of teaching, due simply to students' engagement by the topic.

And again, lest you feel awed by my massive erudition, let me confess that it took me perhaps as much as an hour to find an historical example to illustrate the theorem (located in Pappas, 1989). Then I spent about twenty minutes looking up Eratosthenes in an encyclopaedia and a classical dictionary. This easily gathered knowledge provided the framing for the stark theorem that can serve to humanize it and embed it in an accessibly meaningful context.

Science

With the growing concern about environmental issues there has been evident an increasing focus on topics such as the one I will deal with here — "Trees". I will assume that this topic is being taught at the upper end of the age-range, and so I will build into its narrative structure some general ideas. Let us take the categories of the framework, then, and see how they help us shape the topic for teaching.

Identifying Transcendent Qualities

How can we identify transcendent human qualities in trees? We think of trees as providing our chief building materials and fuel (remembering also that coal is made from trees that decayed during the lush carboniferous period); they yield pulp for paper; they produce edible fruits and nuts; they give off oxygen which we require for life and absorb the carbon dioxide which we exhale; their roots conserve water and prevent soil erosion; and they provide homes for a vast array of animals and insects. Trees are thus crucial to our lives, to the structure of our world, and to the fabric of our civilization. We might then choose as a usable transcendent quality faithful supportiveness. That is, we will see trees in terms of the faithful support they have constantly given to human beings and human civilizations. One of the themes to be brought out by this choice will be how we respond to this faithful supportiveness.

What affective <u>image</u> is evoked by seeing trees in the role of faithful supporters? If we consider the prolific diversity of trees and their appearance around the world in endless shapes and sizes, and how people, poets in particular, use them to represent human moods — the tranquil peace of a tall tree on a summer's evening, the anger of wind-swept trees in riot, and so on — and how they supply ideal building materials and fruit and so many other constituents of our civilizations, we find them tangled in every aspect of our lives and history. An image that catches some of this, quite a common image in the Middle Ages, is one in which we see our different cultures through the ages and across the world nestled in the branches of some great tree. Closely related cultures spread across individual branches; the trunk can be Time; more recent cultures are growing in the canopy, enjoying the sun of the present. Each culture can be seen using the tree to build, to carve, to make utensils, to burn — with its obvious dangers — and some do greater or lesser damage to the great tree; but lives of every culture — kind or cruel — are dependent on it. As teachers, we can encourage our students to elaborate the image to whatever extent seems useful.

The sense of trees' faithful supportiveness provides a transcendent quality with which students will likely find it easy to associate. Our affective theme will centre on what trees do for us, and what we in return do for (or, more commonly, to) trees.

Organizing the Content into a Narrative Structure

We are asked to provide students with <u>initial access to the topic</u> by <u>introducing content that</u> is distinct <u>from their everyday</u> <u>experience but which catches the transcendent quality we will build</u> <u>our narrative on.</u> One way of doing this might be to have students look at human civilizations in what may initially seem a rather odd way. That is, we can see the growth of civilizations as due to their exploiting the faithful supportiveness of trees, and the decline of civilizations as due to their having done so to excess, exhausting the supply.

To take just the familiar outline narrative of Western history, we can recast it in a quite different light, or take a new perspective on it. So we will see the Sumerian Kingdom of Mesopotamia as owing much of its wealth to its learning to exploit its great cedars. After nearly a thousand years, the Sumerian civilization came to an ignominious end due to over-vigorous logging. The fruitful agricultural valleys were ruined by salts eroded from the denuded hills. In similar vein, we can trace the rise and fall of all the ancient civilizations in terms of their access to trees. Athens, for example, rose on the power it gained through the ships produced from the forests of Attica, and fell as that reliable source of timber was destroyed by the Spartans during the Peloponnesian war. The Roman Empire collapsed as it could no longer support its legions in the North and East. That support relied very heavily on silver from Spanish mines. The silver was not exhausted, but it could no longer be smelted because the Roman furnaces had consumed five hundred million trees and laid waste seven thousand square miles of productive forests. The burst of Tudor economic development, and the basis for England's maritime Empire, was laid by Robert Cecil's giving trading monopolies only to English-built ships. This led to the rapid depletion of oak forests for ship-building, but it also stimulated related activities such as glass-blowing and iron-smelting. Through the following couple of centuries the forested island of Britain was laid almost bare. In three decades around the Civil War, the ten thousand hectare Forest of Dean was reduced by 1667 to just a couple of hundred trees. Britain's fate did not so quickly follow that of earlier empires only because of the invention of the coking process for coal and the rise of steam power. Similarly, the U.S.A., "an almost universal forest" as a French visitor described it shortly after Independence, saw its woodlands fuel the needs of farmers and burgeoning industry, of steamships and railroads. Coal, again, maintained American economic and political power for some time.

The rise and fall of the civilizations of the ancient and early modern worlds can generally be told in terms of their exploitation and exhaustion of timber. And today, economic growth in many Third World countries is still being fueled by the consumption of tropical rain forests. What is being done in the Amazon is being done in British Columbia, and has been done throughout the ages. Trees have faithfully supported the growth of civilizations, and those who have abused this faithful support have been destroyed as a result. Perhaps we are now seeing this same cycle on a planetary scale. In such a context it becomes a bit futile for the wealthy countries, whose power was gained by exploiting and destroying their own forests, to lecture Third World countries who are only following their example.

This introductory perspective can be taught using whatever methods individual teachers think best, from exposition to guided imagery, or by mixing a number of methods. (Again, lest it be assumed that I have vast knowledge to draw on, I might mention that all the information above, and what follows, comes from a single book review — Stephen Mills's [1990] review of John Perlin's *A Forest Journey: The Role of Wood in the Development of Civilization*, New York: Norton, 1990, and from the usual half hour with the encyclopaedia.) This whole introductory theme, while appealing to developing "philosophic" interests in students, has within it an expression of extreme behaviours — greed going so far as to undermine what supplies its desires. It expresses the same moral as the story of killing the goose that laid the golden eggs.

On what clear narrative structure will we build knowledge about trees? We could develop our opening theme and follow an historical outline, looking at the different trees used in different civilizations and the varied purposes they were used for. This would focus us on the characteristics of various trees, their typical environmental conditions, the qualities of their woods, the varied uses made of them — from building, to fuel, to toys, to art. That is, I think it would be possible to use the dramatic and unconventional tree-centred view of history as a workable narrative structure. To do this adequately, however, one would need quite a lot of information. (One would have to read Perlin's book, not merely a review of it!) Assuming that I am having to plan the unit with my limited knowledge of trees, I might prefer a different narrative structure that will focus students on a more general range of knowledge of trees and their faithful supportiveness. As faithful supportiveness is our chosen transcendent quality, it will need to be foremost in our narrative. At its simplest, we could consider the range of ways in which trees are faithfully supportive. But we need some narrative principle that will give a sense of coherent and meaningful movement through that range. If all inspiration fails, we can organize our theme on something like size, beginning with the smallest trees and the ways they are faithfully supportive to whichever people, gradually working up to the biggest trees and their uses. Or we could move from the hardest woods to the softest, or follow scientific classifications of trees.

A bit better, however, would be a narrative structure that has a central affective component. We might in such a case see trees as involved in struggles between conditions which favour their growth and spread, and those which threaten them. It is clear where the humans whom they faithfully support would feature in this scenario. Alternatively, a narrative which was structured by the degrees of trees' faithful supportiveness to humans could work. We could even take a scheme like Maslow's "hierarchy of needs" (1970) and show how trees contribute to each need — from oxygen for life itself to toys or equipment for our self-fulfilling play. One might pick up the historical theme from the introduction and look at the contributions of trees to human life from the earliest food and construction materials to the most modern. The narrative we choose will be determined by the requirement that we teach about the biology of trees, their variety, and their environmental roles.

The affective component, however, can be injected by responding to the remaining questions in the framework, even if our narrative structure is as stark as moving from the roots of the tree and working up the trunk to the branches and foliage. We could concentrate on each in turn, considering the variety of forms in different trees, and build our unit around the faithful supportiveness of each part. Let us take this simple narrative structure for our unit.

So we will see the tree, like any living thing, designed to reproduce itself. The roots hold it in place and get the required nutrients, the trunk is to raise the reproductive parts and expose them to pollination and the leaves to light for photosynthesis. The trunk also moves water and other nutrients up and moves food down to the roots for storage and for use as growth tissue.

We are next asked a series of questions, answering which should ensure that we "humanize" the content of our unit. We begin by considering how the content can be shown in terms of human hopes, fears, intentions, and other emotions. In the case of trees I think this is rather easy, especially given the basic transcendent quality that is directing our focus. We will learn about root systems and trunks and leaves and fruit in terms of the ways they support various human hopes, fears, intentions, and so on. This can be made easier by using case studies occasionally. Consider, for example, a tribe whose life is intricately bound up with the fruit and wood products derived from particular trees.

What aspects of the content can best stimulate romance, wonder, and awe? We might deploy a considerable amount of knowledge about trees in order to respond to this question. Romance and wonder can be stimulated by knowledge of the strangest or most exotic trees, by peculiar life cycles or extreme attainments. Students might, again, compile a "book of records" noting the Pacific Coast redwoods as the tallest trees reaching over 105 metres; the giant sequoias as the most massive; the Japanese trained bonsai as the smallest; the Mexican swamp cypress extending to 50 metres in circumference; the bristlecone pines in Nevada being the oldest living things on earth, reaching 4,600 years; and the double cocoanut that is native to a couple of tiny islands in the Seychelles, whose fruit takes 10 years to mature and reaches 20 kilos in weight. One can look at the oddest trees, like the mangrove, the South American ombu, the Madagascar traveller's tree, or the talipot palm of Asia — which grows steadily for about 75 years and then bursts into glorious flower and dies. Students might discover how many seeds a young pine gives off in a year or the number of species of flowering trees there are.

While studying the trunk, one might wonder at the "workability" of wood, considering the remarkable technology developed to respond to this central feature of trees' faithful supportiveness — at the tools for cutting and shaping wood, drying it and treating it against decay; at the endless ingenious fastening devices, screws, and nails that help to restructure wood into new shapes and purposes. Awe might be encouraged by asking each student to write a one-year biography of a particular tree. During that time they could produce a book with photographs, measurements, poems, information, and drawings of "their" tree.

It may seem obvious that one can readily locate ideals and revolts against conventions in this topic. The realization of the exhaustibility of trees, the destruction of species, the elimination of forests, and the impact of all this on the ecosystem provides an ideal of conservation and good management of trees, one that runs counter to the convention of thoughtless exploitation which has prevailed for so long. Our historical introduction has laid the ground for this on the basis of simple self-interest. But our ideal may take us beyond self-interest towards an ideal of shared life; trees were not made for us but we share a planet and ideally our lives contribute to each other's. The relationship between trees and humans is distinctly unequal. They need us much less than we need them.

But another, unconventional, way of seeing trees in revolt against conventions could be to consider their long resistance to classification. This begins with the inability to give a precise definition of "tree". There is such a gradual change from the paradigmatic trees to shrubs to herbaceous plants that one cannot draw a clear line. The problems continue with attempts to classify kinds of trees. General distinctions between softwoods (conifers) and hardwoods (dicotyledons) become distinctly unuseful when we have to classify balsa, the softest of all woods, as a hardwood. "Evergreen" and "deciduous" turn out to be less than useful categories when we realize that whether or not some species retain their foliage in winter is due to climatic conditions. In the process of studying the greater or lesser adequacy of various classificatory schemes in this context students should learn a considerable amount about the various terms and names given to kinds of trees.

The pursuit of detailed knowledge about some particular tree, or part of trees, or process of growth, or whatever, can be given to small groups of students for the period of the unit. If the task of writing a one-year biography of a tree is given, then that should satisfy this item. The aim is to enable students to develop as exhaustive as possible an understanding of some aspect of the topic, to give them a sense of the security that can come with knowing as much about something as possible. We want to help students get some sense of the scale of the phenomenon they are learning about.

Concluding

An excellent conclusion for this unit would be to tell or read or watch the animated film of Jean Giono's *The Man Who Planted Trees* (National Film Board of Canada). Giono tells of his walking as a young man in a desolated region in the south of France and eventually, worried about lack of water and food, meeting a shepherd. During the evening the shepherd carefully sorted a dozen acorns, and the next day he planted them. Giono stayed a few days, and each day the shepherd planted more acorns. The story of Elzéard Bouffier, the shepherd, covers forty years, during which, interrupted by wars and his own marriage and family life, Giono occasionally revisits him. Over the years of planting trees, woods sprout and grow and eventually forests thrive. They retain water, and so streams flow again where earlier there had long been dry beds, and people come back to the deserted villages and rebuild. Bouffier, by slowly planting trees day by day, brought back thronging life to what had been a rocky desert. (This film, available as a video-cassette, won an Oscar for its vivid re-creation of the story.)

Evaluation

We can, again, use whatever traditional evaluation procedures seem appropriate to discover whether students have learned the basic knowledge concerning trees. We will also want to observe their work on the biography of "their" tree, to try to assess whether it has helped stimulate any sense of awe. Their enthusiasm for accumulating knowledge of strange trees, of processes of growth, or of peculiar adaptations can serve as an index of the degree to which the topic has engaged their sense of wonder. Their sense of a balanced ecological ideal of good management of trees can indicate the degree to which they have developed an understanding of trees' role in the environment. Teachers' sensitivity to such dimensions of students' engagement with the topic can provide an imprecise but very real evaluation of how far they are being successful in stimulating students' imaginations, arboreally.

Social Studies

In many ways social studies content seems relatively easy to shape according to the categories of the framework. As a subject area, it is made up of what John Dewey called people's associated life. It is an area in which people's intentions, emotions, conflicts, and so on, form a prominent part of its subject matter. During the period of students' school lives which forms the focus of this book, history and geography become central to most social studies curricula. History is clearly amenable to the framework and as geography is increasingly taught as "human geography", as an interaction between people and environment, so too it seems to present little resistance to being shaped by the framework's questions. While various reports suggest that history, geography, and social studies in general are commonly presented in ways that very largely fail to engage students' imaginations, nevertheless it may seem that compared with mathematics and science it should prove relatively easy to structure social studies knowledge according to the principles and framework developed earlier. I'm not sure this is the case. I suspect it may seem easier because one can more easily develop a narrative involving people, but, in doing so, teachers may well neglect those other principles that give romantic perspective and imaginative energy to a narrative.

For the social studies example to be articulated according to the framework let me take "Government". I choose this only because last night I was doing a workshop with a group of social studies teachers, discussing a version of the framework and its underlying principles. At the conclusion of my expository part, the teachers suggested topics, and we worked out how they could be shaped and presented in imaginatively engaging ways. Mostly this went well; it was easy to show how the structuring of material by the traditional objectives/content/methods/evaluation scheme produced one kind of useful ordering, and that reformulating the material in terms of this framework's questions produced a rather different ordering that seemed likely to convey the information at least as well and also be more imaginatively engaging. Unfortunately it was not till time was running out that I had the idea of asking for topics which the teachers found the dullest and most difficult to teach. One teacher immediately called out "Government", to general laughter and agreement. We had only time to begin thinking about it, so let me try to deal with it here. No doubt some readers might find Government an intrinsically interesting topic with which they routinely have success, readily stimulating students' imaginations, but it was clear that nearly all the teachers I was with last night found it difficult to make the topic engaging.

Identifying Transcendent Qualities

The first step again is to identify transcendent qualities within the topic. In the sense suggested earlier, what do we pick out when examining "Government" with our affective sensors alert? Consider what democratic government is and how it has evolved. We see it usually in terms of politicians, bureaucrats, and institutions, with their ceremonies and programmes, of elections and lobbying, of ideas of representation and ideals of democracy, and of a lot of mess, clutter, and inefficiency. The dullness of the topic felt by the teachers I met with last night was due, I think, to their seeing it very largely, and certainly primarily, in terms of content. There is indeed some tedium in laying out as objectives that students learn about the various institutions of government and their roles, when the teacher feels constrained from dealing also with the mess, clutter, and inefficiency which forms a vivid part of the topic in the actual lives of the teachers. It is not so much that they feel able to teach only an ideal of how government works, but rather that it is not an ideal in the romantic sense discussed earlier, but instead one that is disconnected from much of the reality that gives the topic its life and energy.

But if we approach it affectively, we can make our focus whatever gives off that sense of life and energy. One way, picking up from the point about mess, clutter, and inefficiency, would be to see "Government" as a triumphant organization of endless conflicting greeds, power struggles, self-interests, competing lobbies, and so on. But that would bring into the foreground much of the content that some teachers feel wary of. Let us consider an alternative that might be less problematic and still capable of getting at some of the life and energy in the topic. There are, after all, many transcendent qualities within any complex topic.

We can, for example, see democratic government as a set of wonderful achievements that have required and require courage, forbearance, tolerance, and so on. Government is also an embodiment of emotions, of people's hopes, fears and ambitions. It works only by the consent of millions of individuals who forgo some of their desires and interests for the benefit of some larger group. It serves as a control mechanism, preventing the strong from wholly exploiting the weak, and struggling to provide relative security against arbitrary violence. Democratic government is the device invented so that individuals can pursue their interests and try to fulfil their hopes and ambitions, while at the same time it attempts to ensure that no one person or group intrudes excessively on the aspirations of others. That government works by a mass of compromises — commonly stumbling inefficiently from initiative to initiative, each undermined or altered to fit some "selfish" interest — and that it provides a public arena for ambition born of personal insecurity and greed for money and power, needs to be present in our unit; but we have to try to find the more profound positive emotions that keep democratic governments afloat. The wonder of democratic government is that it does not flail into chaos but manages among the changing, warring, thronging human desires and passions to ensure its citizens' survival and the pursuit of their wishes.

Having ranged across the topic with our affective sensors alert, we are asked the related question of what affective image they can evoke. Here we will look for something central to the topic, something general that can encompass all the content we will want students to learn. Again, we could evoke many images. What we can do is relax, and let those affective elements and the transcendent qualities we have identified suggest their own image: so that seething mass of conflicting hopes and ambitions, which seems in constant danger of falling into chaos, manages somehow to stagger forward, helping people to live the lives they want; so that we might find forming in our minds the image of a well-meaning but unstable giant, carrying a population on a huge tray, contoured and shaped like the country, constantly stumbling and zig-zagging, trying to follow the directions given by the people being carried. The giant has to struggle over treacherous terrain — buffeted, abused, despised — yet persisting. The people on the tray ignore him, getting on with their lives, but occasionally shout for him to turn right, or left, or go back, or leap forward. Much of his stumbling is due to trying to follow all these directions at once. And yet the giant keeps going, more or less forward, and manages to stay upright, and keep the country more or less on an even keel.

The giant is "Government", and it gives us an image in which we can identify transcendent qualities with which students could associate. We could identify many qualities, depending on how we want to present the topic. For immediate purposes let us focus on the courage and generosity of spirit that are evident in our giant and are necessary for a democratic government to work. We might not see these at all in some politicians or bureaucrats, or see them only some of the time in others, but they exist in many people in varying degrees at different times, and in the population at large in varying degrees at different times. Given our educational purpose, of course, it might be no bad thing to make clear to students that some courage and generosity of spirit are important constituents of democratic governments and of citizens in a democracy.

Well, I have used a few pages laying out a kind of meditation on this first step and you have spent a few minutes reading it. (Thank you!) After a bit of experience focussing on transcendent qualities and evoking images from them, this step need take no more than a few seconds. Certainly I have simply taken the first transcendent qualities and the first image that came to mind, intent on showing how the framework functions rather than on producing a stellar unit-plan. This first step involves the kind of thinking that can be carried on in the car on the way to school or at night just before going to sleep or whenever. It seems possible that it might be most effective when the mind is relaxed, perhaps half engaged with other things.

Organizing the Content into a Narrative Structure

I will be focussing here on the principles whereby we shape the topic "Government" into a clear and coherent narrative that stimulates students' imaginations.

The framework suggests that our first focus should not be on the overall narrative structure but rather on how we should provide access to the topic. It suggests further that we should look for something dramatically different from students' everyday experience. It must also catch as vividly as possible the transcendent qualities, in this case, of courage and generosity of spirit. One alternative that might serve us well here is the image or images we formed earlier. If we have successfully caught some transcendent qualities in our image, then that image might provide an appropriate means of access for students.

Let us, then, use the image of the courageous and generous-spirited giant that represented our first affective association with the transcendent qualities we identified in "Government". The teacher can evoke — by whatever method seems best — the image of the giant staggering along carrying the country as far as possible in the direction most people are shouting for. This could be elaborated considerably to provide a fair analogy with the government's structure. So the teacher, or the student, might suggest a perch near the giant's ear on which a small group selected from the people below were carried in some comfort. They are the ones who mostly tell the giant what direction to go in, and how fast or slow. But they confuse the giant by shouting different things and changing their minds at irregular intervals. Also, shouts from the people below sometimes drown out the select group. At regular intervals the group by his ear all climb down and wander about the country asking the people to let them back into the comfortable seats by the giant's ear. Some come back to their seats, others don't, and new people take their places. We can elaborate the drama further by having the giant be required to help other giants carrying other countries or having him trip others, and so on. The teacher and students could expand the image to incorporate as many of the features of "Government" as they can think of. It is important, if we are to follow the framework, to ensure that the giant is perceived as a courageous figure, showing generosity of spirit.

Having introduced the topic in such a way that students are confronted by some dramatic image that engages their association with courage and generosity of spirit, we are asked by the framework to structure the body of the unit or lesson into a clear narrative. What is the plot-line or story-line that our unit on Government is to take? There could, of course, be many different structures. In most places, particularly in the U.S.A., this topic appears in curricula not just so that students can learn about different forms of government but rather, primarily, so that they will learn about their own. So our narrative structure will have to allow for this requirement.

We could choose an historical narrative line. Doing so would allow us to examine the fate of different forms of government throughout history, considering the ways and degrees in which they required courage and generosity of spirit. This might be done relatively briefly, highlighting with vivid anecdotes some of the exotic features of different governmental systems through the ages. Again, this need not be trivial; the task is to locate events and characters that show both distinctive features of the form of government and the degrees of courage and generosity of spirit it required or encouraged.

Alternatively, one could look at forms of government on a continuum of courage and generosity of spirit, either disregarding historical period or dealing only with contemporary examples. So one might begin with an extreme in which these transcendent qualities seem to have been almost entirely absent, such as certain dictatorships or, say, Ceausescu's Romania. Then one can give examples along the continuum, moving perhaps to the other extreme where we find the most tolerant democracies — in which diversity is encouraged and the rights of distinct groups to be different are upheld by the government and by the people's clear support of its tolerant policies.

This kind of narrative line does not require that we spend equal amounts of time on all parts of it; its purpose is to enable us to structure our content into a kind of story. The curriculum may require us to spend nearly all our time on the details of our own country's governmental structure, but this does not prevent us setting it within a wider context. In one of the cases that we might use, the transcendent qualities of courage and generosity of spirit will be associated clearly with the greater degree of democracy evident in governments. So what we additionally achieve here is not to set up our own form of government as the object of students' affective associations, but to establish courage and generosity of spirit as the object of their associations. "Our" government, then, may benefit from the students' affective associations to the degree that it is seen to embody those transcendent qualities.

Having decided on a narrative line, on a sense of coherent movement through the unit, we are now asked to attend to humanizing its content. There are numerous ways we can do this. If, for example, we want to describe the role of the legal system in our government, we might use one or more case studies. So instead of simply naming, defining and describing the various parts of the legal system, with diagrams and flowcharts perhaps, we might take the real or invented case of an individual with a particular grievance he or she takes to law.

It will be important, to respond to the question in the framework, to see the circumstances of the case study through the emotions of the individuals involved — their hopes, fears, sense of injustice, and whatever else. We can then follow the adventures of this individual through the legal system, learning about it through our character's experiences and emotional responses to them. It would obviously be sensible to choose a case that is not decided simply, but one that follows a trail of appeals to the highest courts in the country. At the end of this case study, or after a few case studies, students can then move towards systematizing the knowledge they will have learned, and at this point the diagrams and flowcharts are likely to make better sense.

A part of the humanizing process, the framework suggests, is to bring out aspects of our topic that stimulate romance, wonder, and awe. (I tend to think that this last and rare emotion is perhaps the easiest to evoke in the case of "Government". Given the riot of ambitions, greed, disregard for the rights of others, intolerance, and blind self-interest that seem so common in our democracies, the fact that our systems of government manage to carry on at all inspires awe. Perhaps this is too cynical a view, but even so some sense of it seems an appropriate part of our unit: that despite the weaknesses of individuals our systems of government struggle on, upholding higher values than many of its agents hold. This is an important and somewhat awe-inspiring feature of democratic government.)

Romance might be engaged again by case studies or biographies of people who have played significant roles in democratic governments and who most clearly exemplify in their lives the virtues of courage and generosity of spirit. One thinks of figures like Ghandi, but there are very many people who have performed and continue to perform better than we have a right to expect in giving active life to the chosen transcendent qualities. This is not a call to make heroes out of particular men and women active in government, but rather to see their activities as showing students something further about how their government works and about the human qualities that are desirable for it to work well.

The sheer complexity of much modern government activity can stimulate wonder through the truly astounding statistics that it yields. Students might be encouraged to contribute to a "wonder-board" — though it might wisely be called something more like "Governments' Records". Students could seek statistics about, for example, how much land the government owns; how many people it employs; how much paper it consumes in a month, week, or day, and what acreage of forest is required to supply that amount; which government is the richest and which the poorest; what proportion of their populations different state, provincial, or local governments employ; how many laws govern its activities.

The final question in this step of the framework asks us to consider ideals and revolts against convention. We have touched on ideals above, so we might for a moment consider revolt, because usually government represents the conventions people sometimes revolt against. What we are invited to consider here is how governments respond to revolts against some of their entrenched conventions. We might again use particular case studies. In the

U.S.A. we might consider the case of the Civil Rights movement and Martin Luther King; in Canada, say, the demands of French-speaking Quebec; in Britain, the demands of the work force for social services, such as health and education, run by the government; and equivalent cases in other places. These examples each show people who have some legitimate claim against their government. (This is not to say that we must wholeheartedly agree with any of these groups to recognize that they have *some* grounds for feeling that their government is not showing either courage or generosity of spirit in its dealings with them.) We may observe how some conventions harden over time, until the transcendent qualities we are looking for in government seem to be eroded. The qualities might then be more evident in those who revolt against the government. In many cases in democracies we will see the result of the revolt being a recognition of the legitimate claim of those in revolt and, when courage and generosity of spirit are shown by those in government dealing with such claims, we see a mechanism whereby democracies can renew themselves. The transcendent qualities expressed by citizens in revolt can come to be a part of the government over time.

The final part of this step of the framework asks us to consider what parts of our unit on government are amenable to exhaustively detailed study. This might seem the easiest question to satisfy, as students can be given almost any aspect of the topic on which to prepare a project, either individually or in groups. But this question is a little harder to satisfy, I think, than may at first seem the case. Not that it is particularly difficult, but it is slightly problematic finding aspects of the topic which are "exhaustible". Looking in detail at the structure of central government departments or the legal system or local government, can just be too vague, and leave the student with something that is not exhaustible in any useful sense. It will usually be better to focus more precisely on something more specific. Which government officials meet on a daily basis with the President or Prime Minister? What steps did three members of the legislature go through in order to reach their present positions? What steps does a new law have to go through before it is enacted?

My point here is simply to note the preference, in this framework, for something that students can exhaust. Not that this, or any other of these features, should be taken as an iron-clad rule. It is a principle with what seems some significant value for practice. Clearly there will be cases when "inexhaustible" topics can profitably be pursued in detail, and occasions when exhaustible topics can be trivial. But if the general principle is borne in mind, teachers can use it where it seems of most value.

Concluding

How can we bring the unit on "Government" to a satisfactory closure? This does not mean "closing off", but rather engaging in some activity that draws together in some general way the content of the unit. This can often be done in showing how, once the material has been learned, it can become the basis for further interesting explorations. One shows that this is not just a unit of content to be acquired before moving on to the next, but that understanding it opens one to further understanding and brings within one's power a wider range of questions — questions which can now have a fuller meaning.

For example, one might use the knowledge gained about democratic government to consider what might be done about the immense diversity of wealth available in democracies and the enormous inequalities this leads to in access to education, in health care, and in various kinds of freedom. At what point does trying to ensure greater equality undercut the form of democratic government we have, and at what point does the degree of inequality undercut the form of democratic government we have?

Again, teachers can pose such questions using any of a wide range of methods, from class discussions, to inquiry procedures, to simulations, to guided discovery scenarios. Whatever method is chosen, however, the point is to focus on some significant question about government that students can feel some satisfaction in dealing with because it requires that they deploy the knowledge they have gained through the unit. Such questions make new and important sense to them.

Evaluation

We might use any of the usual forms of evaluation to ensure that students understand the nature of their government and know its composition, the relationships of its parts, and so on. Such evaluations may come from regular examinations of students' knowledge, and from the various projects they would have done during the unit, including perhaps their own exhaustive exploration of some detailed aspect of government.

Because this unit has been trying to engage students' imaginations with the topic, we will also want to evaluate how successful we have been in this regard. We obviously do not have well-tried and tested evaluation procedures that will give us precise readings of imaginative engagement, and probably never will have. At this stage we would do well to experiment with methods that seem plausible. One general procedure, of course, is teachers' observation. It is usually fairly clear whether students are imaginatively engaged or not in a topic. Also their written work, or other forms of presentation, can give evidence of imaginative engagement. Most crudely it may be evident when students do more than is required of them and particularly when their additional work takes off at an angle determined by their own interests. It may be evident in the care and concern that goes into the work. (These latter could also be caused by other things too, like desire for a grade or compulsion. But it is an unusually unobservant teacher who cannot tell the difference.) In addition, of course, teachers might draw on the procedures referred to above in Guba and Lincoln (1981) and Patton (1990).

When I mentioned "other forms of presentation" above, I was thinking that, in classrooms where students do become imaginatively engaged and in which the imagination is clearly valued in learning, the ways in which students are either encouraged by imaginative teachers or stimulated by their own imaginations to present their own work to the class tends to be unconventional. I have seen groups who have studied specific science topics in detail deliver their presentations to the class in rap-songs which they composed. The evaluation here involved both the scientific content — which tended to be very accurate —

and the vividness with which they conveyed it and conveyed why it mattered.

Language Arts

It would appear that material in Language Arts most readily lends itself to a treatment designed to engage students' imaginations. The Arts, after all, are the areas in which, it is commonly assumed, imagination finds its proper and fullest expression. One theme of this book has been to contest this assumption: to argue that imagination ought to be seen as no less at home in, and requiring engagement and expression in, mathematics and science curricula. Because the assumption has been so prevalent, mathematics and science are more commonly taught in ways that do not have strong and widely practiced traditions of engaging the imagination — despite the efforts of many imaginative teachers in those areas. Consequently, notwithstanding the fact that much of this framework simply tries to systematize what I have seen many good mathematics and science teachers do, applying the framework to such areas tends to produce organizations of topics that are unlike much current practice. Because Language Arts has been conventionally assumed to be constantly engaging students' imaginations, it may be expected that application of this framework will bring about less dramatic changes from those currently common. Let us see if this is the case.

As I have been choosing from other curriculum areas topics which on first look might not seem particularly hospitable to imaginative engagement, let me here choose a topic that might seem in need of no help from a framework such as that above. My local curriculum, randomly opened, recommends a unit on a corpus of myth stories. Let me arbitrarily select the Norse from the set indicated, and see what the framework can do to help us organize it.

Identifying Transcendent Qualities

The Norse myths — like any corpus of myths — embody a huge range of transcendent qualities — courage, wisdom, beauty, compassion, etc. How can we apply this first category to the topic, then? An implication of the framework is that coherence in the unit turns in some degree on focussing on some central transcendent quality. As in an engaging story one cannot have a number of plots and themes running at the same time, so in a unit of study which is to be imaginatively engaging we should begin by deciding on a focal transcendent quality on which we will, as it were, hang the topic. The quality I will choose in this case — and there could be a number of others depending on how one wants initially to present Norse mythology — is that of doomed courage, beauty, and wisdom, what might be called a kind of stoic melancholy. The gods of Asgard fight against forces of chaos and ice, against destructive monsters, against the wiles of the renegade Loki, while knowing all along that they will be required to meet, in the final battle of the Ragnarok, accumulated foes who will defeat them.

The myths are full of images that catch this transcendent quality. Loki fathered three monsters, among them the fearsome Fenris-Wolf with teeth like swords and eyes of flame. The gods tried to bind him with ropes and chains but he broke out of them with ease. So they tried to trick him into being bound by the slender but unbreakable thread, Gleipner, made by dwarves from the footfall of a cat, a woman's beard, the roots of a mountain, the nerves of a bear, the breath of a fish, and the spittle of a bird. But Fenris-Wolf was distrustful of this slender thread. Tyr, the god of War, put his sword-bearing right wrist into Fenris-Wolf's mouth saying, "If the bond is enchanted, my hand is forfeit". Fenris-Wolf allowed himself to be bound, and could not break free. Tyr never tried to move his hand. Then the wolf fell still. Monster and war god, face to face, were silent. Fenris in cold and bitter anger snapped his foam-flecked teeth and tore off the god's right hand.

Organizing the Content into a Narrative Structure

Norse myth stories are many, but the general recommendation of the framework is that we do not simply expose students to them as a set of good stories that they might enjoy, but rather that we see the whole corpus of Norse mythology as an overall narrative articulated, in this case, on the transcendent quality of stoic melancholy in the face of doomed courage, beauty, and wisdom.

For initial access, then, we might use the story of Tyr. Our telling should emphasize the transcendent quality we have identified as central to the Norse corpus. That emphasis may be made more pronounced by making clear that this attempt to rein in the fearsome Fenris-Wolf was seen even at the time as a temporary restraint, and that Fenris-Wolf will tear free at the Ragnarok, devouring even Allfather Odin.

How can we shape a clear narrative line from the great diversity of Norse myths? We can try to show a pattern that stretches between the beginning and the end of the Norse gods (and I will draw on such a retelling of these myths by Susanna Egan). So we might begin with the nightmares of Balder the Beautiful, son of Odin and best loved of all the gods in Asgard, god of light and the green springtime. He lies sick with grief, and the other gods of Asgard are afraid. Odin rides on Sleipnir, his eight-legged horse, out of Asgard, over the rainbow bridge, to the depths of earth, to the gloomy halls of Hel, goddess of the dead.

He calls by powerful spells the Wise Woman from the dead. Odin had given an eye for memory, for knowledge of the past, and the Wise Woman knew the future. She will tell Odin the future, and the fate of Balder and of Asgard, only if he will first tell her of the beginning of the world. She warns Odin that she will only fill his heart with sorrow, but as he had given an eye for knowledge of the past so he would bear whatever was necessary also to know the future.

He tells of the beginning of the yawning abyss, Ginnungagap, in the creaking ice and misty night, and the fire from the south which melts it, giving birth to Ymir and his offspring, the Giants. He tells, too, of the birth of gods and of men and all the other creatures who live on the earth. In return the Wise Woman tells of Ragnarok, and the breaking free of all the monsters and horrors the gods had held in check, and how the evil cunning of Loki will be used to kill Balder, though every living thing, except the mistletoe, had vowed to protect him, and how the ice and chaos would come again. But in the end a new world would arise, and human beings would find the golden chessmen that the gods had played with in the summer days of their rule scattered in the grass.

This sketch of an overall narrative provides a context within which the various myth stories that will form the content of our unit can find place and added meaning, and can be constantly connected with the general transcendent quality of stoic melancholy. This does not mean that each individual story can only express this quality. Rather each story, whatever other qualities it articulates, can find a place in the overall pattern, and can both contribute something to the sense of stoic melancholy and receive an additional layer of meaning from it. Following the framework, then, suggests that we establish first an overall narrative structure from earliest ice to the Ragnarok, and beyond, and see the time of the gods between this beginning and end as a struggle for courage, beauty, and wisdom in the face of evil monsters, trickery, and terrible natural forces.

Humanizing the content in this unit should require little work. The stories are built from powerful human emotions. If teachers want to retell the stories, they might usefully consider as a model the work of Barbara Leonie Picard (1953). She chooses the vivid details that fix characters and dramatize events, and focusses constantly on transcendent qualities and human emotions.

Romance and wonder are evoked continually by the various stories. The adventures of Odin, Freya, Thor, Loki, and the other gods of Asgard are vivid and, to the modern student, exotic and strange. They add a dimension to our experience and enlarge our grasp on the world — a function of all great literature. Awe might be stimulated by pulling back at some moment or moments during the unit and reflecting on the people who spun these complex and moving stories. They have a unique and immensely evocative overall tone or emotional resonance. We might also try to have students imagine, with the help of as much information as possible of course, the role of these stories in the lives of the people for whom they formed a core of their living culture.

One of the ideals which the overall narrative highlights is courage in the face of sure destruction. It generates a sense of melancholy that does not yield to despair, but rather supports energetic activity. Conventionally, assurance of the failure of hopes leads to lassitude and despair. What we associate with in the Norse gods is energetic activity and a joy in life itself and in our powers to fight for the good and beautiful even when our cause is hopeless. We will all die, but while we live we should live with energy and courage, beauty and wisdom; this is an ideal powerfully represented in these stories.

There are two sets of details that might be pursued in this unit. One concerns the contents of the stories, the other their context. Students might, for example, focus on individual characters, composing as complete a biography of, say, Balder or Freya or Odin as can be constructed from the corpus. Alternatively, students might look in detail at the period when the stories were written down, what form they took, what is known of their historical background, and so on.

Concluding

A range of powerful themes recur in Norse myths, and our conclusion might involve making the main ones explicit after students have become familiar with a significant set of the stories. We might focus on, for example, the theme of mortality that underlies the myths. All myth corpuses seem to have accounts of why people must die, and their death is usually tied up intricately with their creation; in our beginning is our end. We might again draw a connecting narrative line between beginnings and ends — of gods and men — and see how the two are tangled together.

Evaluation

What would one seek to evaluate from such a unit? If we want to know whether the students have followed the stories, and can identify Odin, Freya, Thor, the Wise Woman, Hel, Balder, and so on, we could go about discovering that quite easily with traditional evaluation procedures. But we should always ask what effects our forms of evaluation will have on teaching and learning. What, in this case, would such an anticipated examination do to students' sense of the myths? If they are to be evaluated, even if only in part, on their knowledge of who the characters are and on details of the events of the stories, then these will become the focus of students' attention while reading or hearing or dramatizing them.

Evaluation shapes not only teaching, of course, but also students' learning. The problem with this prosaic kind of evaluation for students' study of literature in general is that it directs their attention wrongly. They do not feel with their hearts the melancholy of Norse myths because they are busy trying to fix characters, events, and names in their short-term memories. This, at least, is the kind of interference with a proper imaginative engagement with literature that such evaluations constantly threaten.

Imagine that you are going to see a newly released film that you are sure you will enjoy. You are told that, on coming out of the cinema, you will be given a test to make sure you have learned the names of the characters and their main characteristics, details of their backgrounds and of the events and the locations in which they take place. Your salary will be adjusted according to your performance in the test. Do you imagine that you would straightforwardly enjoy the film? Indeed you would probably conclude that the prospect of a test, on which your future in some way depended, ruined the film for you. If you knew that such a test would follow every film you were to see, you would likely conclude that this would ruin the cinema for you. Yet we do this to students constantly after they read a work of literature. Shakespeare's plays were written to enlarge experience and give pleasure, not to provide detail for exam questions. Current evaluation procedures in schools ensure that the first two intentions are very greatly diminished and the last is made prominent. The results are as predictable as requiring adults to take tests after attending the cinema and adjusting their salaries in accordance with results.

What kind of evaluation is appropriate, then? If our intention is to engage students' imaginations with the transcendent quality of stoic melancholy to extend the range of their emotional sensitivity and human understanding, then it is the degree of our success in achieving this that must be the focus of our evaluation. And if we cannot precisely measure this, we must *not* try to measure something else that seems connected with it, or is a prerequisite or constituent of it — like the names of gods and events of the stories — because then those things will replace our intention as the focus of teaching and learning. We must accept that our evaluation will be imprecise, but we must ensure that it is of a kind that encourages teaching and learning to remain focussed on our primary intention.

The finest instrument we have for evaluating degrees of success in such a unit is the teacher's sensitive observation. This is not, of course, entirely reliable, but at least it does not put reliability of evaluation above the purposes of education. That teachers' sensitivity is our best available evaluation device suggests that some energy might usefully be spent on training it during pre- and in-service professional-development programmes. Eisner, for one, has written persuasively about developing forms of connoisseurship in teachers (1985), and its use in evaluation is clearly important.

If we require "products" that can be evaluated we should ask for those which can display the qualities which the unit was designed to encourage. So we might invite students to write a story that took up similar themes and characters as the myths they had been reading about. Or they might compose stories, poems, plays, improvisations, rap-songs, whatever, that capture the tone of stoic melancholy — locating it in other times and places, and perhaps also in their contemporary experience.

I should add, that while my focus throughout is on teachers' roles, the principles of learning sketched earlier suggest quite strongly that we should also attend to the students' role in evaluation. Because of my focus we have not dwelt much on the nature of students' experience during these examples, though I take it that fairly obvious inferences can be drawn. Students might be expected, imaginatively, to participate in the process of evaluation in all these cases. I have tended to represent them as the passive producers of evidence of their learning, but of course there is also a rich literature in education indicating ways in which they can also be engaged as active evaluators of their own learning (see, e.g., Guba & Lincoln, 1981), and clearly the principles being elaborated above encourage such engagement.

Conclusion

It will be obvious that I think imaginative engagement with mathematics and science content in particular comes most readily by presenting that content in the historical contexts in which it was invented or discovered or had original life. (Though, obviously, this need not be always the case.) This is not so much an argument for a history-based curriculum as it is for seeing knowledge first in the social context in which it has vivid meaning. "Social" is just a general word for the context of human emotions and intentions in terms of which, particularly between ages eight and fifteen, we seem best able to make sense of new content. The key to understanding new material, I am suggesting, is not primarily contact with what is already known, or expansion from the familiar content of one's environment, but is rather embedding it in those contexts of human emotions and intentions that derive meaning from association with transcendent qualities.

Most of the textbooks currently available, of course, do not embody the principles outlined above. Applying this framework, then, will likely require some imaginative activity and perhaps initially a bit of research by teachers, at least with regard to some content. But if these principles come to be taken more seriously, we can expect to see textbooks which will provide appropriate contextual material as well as the basic content.

Perhaps I may say again that I do not see this framework in the rigid format outlined above as a fixture of any teacher's professional tool-kit. Rather I see it as one way in which the principles of imaginative engagement can be articulated as a planning device. Pre-service and in-service teachers might follow it step by step a few times, as just one way in which they might begin to incorporate the principles into their practice. But I anticipate that quite quickly it will be adapted to fit with other techniques and procedures that individual teachers find effective. What I do hope, however, is that the principles — which conflict at a number of points with the dominant principles that affect current practice — will be taken seriously by teachers, and that they will consider their value as against those that seem commonly taken for granted at the moment.

It is perhaps worth noting, incidentally, that the narrative structuring of units seems to lead very easily to a kind of integration across disciplines that some educationalists recommend as desirable. I'm not sure that the framework above necessarily leads to such integration, but it would seem to make it relatively routine.

Conclusion

The latter part of the nineteenth century saw the shaping of a number of the great institutions that remain central to the structure of Western societies. These include the hospital, the prison, the factory, and the school. Each had existed in some form before, of course, but they were each radically transformed during this time to the general condition which has survived to the present. These transformations were guided by a set of ideas which have been carried forward through the years in the institutions they shaped. This set of ideas has also ensured a number of similarities among these institutions.

It is perhaps too easy to exaggerate some of these similarities. The containing and confining function of schools, though likened by some radical writers to that of prisons, is of course un-prisonlike in that it is not intended as a punishment — though children might often take it as such. On the other hand, it is perhaps too easy to dismiss the similarities noted among various of these great social institutions as merely rhetorical. The kind of social positivism that informed James Mill's plans for prisons to shape people and effect improvements in society, and that informed efficient means of mass-producing goods in factories by bringing together component and resources, also left its mark on schools. Occasionally the inadequacy for educational purposes of the ideas that have shaped schools in such a way that they share characteristics with factories and prisons is brought home to us, but for the most part we tend to take as inevitable the organization of large groups of children, divided into sets of age-cohorts, progressing through a curriculum broken into neat chunks, breaking from subject to subject at set time divisions, and so on.

What is not evident in the set of nineteenth-century ideas that have shaped our social institutions is much sense of a place for imagination. Social positivism is surrounded by high-minded, serious, confident, energetic, logical, determined, ameliorative ideas, but little in the way of imagination. The school, as our particular concern, has neither had built into its structure a sense of imagination, nor has had clearly articulated a process whereby it can develop students' imagination. In conclusion, then, I want to consider just a few further implications for teaching and the curriculum if we take imagination seriously in education.

The Role of the Teacher

The factory influence on schooling has left its mark on what is commonly taken to be the role of the teacher. The teacher is considered the agent that serves a process planned and laid-out in government curriculum documents — one which involves taking the unformed child and producing by gradual degrees the knowledgeable, skilled adult who will be economically productive. The training of teachers (and "training", though commonly avoided, is the appropriate term in this model) for furthering this kind of schooling is centrally a matter of inculcating management skills — how to plan lessons and units beginning with objectives, how to "manage" a classroom, and so on. The best teacher-training programmes are thus those that best socialize their students to the prevailing norms of this process.

Now, obviously, given that it is the real world I am trying to write about, such a characterization is simplistic and uni-dimensional. Clearly, throughout the Western world, those students who *additionally* show they can imaginatively engage students are commended and rewarded. The priorities of our teacher-training systems are such that students who are excellent at imaginatively stimulating students but who lack, or choose not to employ, appropriate management skills are likely to find themselves withdrawn from their programmes, failed, not recommended for certification. Students who show not an iota of imagination and who seem guaranteed to bore generations of students mindless but who prove competent users of the approved management skills routinely pass into the teaching profession. Now I am not in favour of poor management skills (!), and draw this parallel only to make the simple point that our system of schooling and the ideas on which it is based consider management skills of more importance than imagination in a teacher. (Questions of how we can assess imaginative ability are quite beside the point here; the fact that there has been no evident interest in such a project in teacher-training programmes is the significant point.)

Another clear feature of imaginative activity is that it is both unpredictable and diverse in each of us. Imaginative development contributes to our diversity rather than to our homogenization. Teachers in an educational system that takes imagination seriously must, then, be accorded a greater degree of autonomy. They cannot be treated as consumers and distributors of the contents of curriculum guides, nor as animated textbooks, nor as worksheet pedlars.

Throughout we have seen connections between imagination and memory. The imagination can work only on what is in the memory, on what one knows. Imaginative life and ignorance are not common companions. The more one knows about something, the more the imagination has to work with. (This is not to say that the more one knows the more imaginative one will be. Knowledge is a necessary but not sufficient condition for imaginative activity.) So whatever difficulties we undoubtedly have in tying "imagination" down precisely, it is nonetheless clear that the "imagination" we have been trying to get clearer about in this book is something that tends to be stimulated by simply knowing a lot about a topic. The more one knows, the easier it is to think of more possibilities. So, one clear conclusion of this discussion of imagination in education is to undermine what is sometimes considered a kind of conflict between "memorizing" lots of history, mathematics, science, and so on, and engaging in a rich imaginative life. The simple conclusion — hardly original, to be sure — is that mastery of disciplined knowledge in a range of curriculum areas properly goes hand in hand with imaginative development.

The implication of this conclusion for teaching and for professional-development programmes is that the more the teacher knows about the subject being taught, the more likely the possibility for imaginative teaching. Put simply this means that teaching is properly a learnèd profession. Too often teachers seem to be expected to display their professionalism by efficient management of large classes or by show-biz performances, rather than by scholarship. Certainly the scholarly virtues are not those most prominent in teacher-training programmes. Nor are they prominent in either the selection of teachers — especially primary teachers where it is crucial — or in in-service training, which tends to favour management techniques over scholarly activities. Well, one can perhaps overdo this point, so that it seems one is asking for something quite impossible. My point is not that we should require a Ph.D. for entry to teaching, but rather that the attitudes of mind that respect and pursue disciplined knowledge, especially in the area of teaching specialty, should be a much more prominent part both of pre-service programmes and of the publicly accepted criteria of what makes teaching a profession rather than a service-industry.

Becoming an evoker and stimulator of imaginations also requires, of course, that the teacher be imaginatively energetic. I believe that this requirement does not make more exhausting a profession that is already draining enough. Some of the current energy-drain is due, I think, to the unindividuated role of teachers as functionaries in some routine production process. It is a process that too rarely returns energy. More imaginative teaching might indeed call for more energy output from teachers, but I think there are abundant examples to show that such teaching generates an invigorating return of energy.

The Imaginative Curriculum

Taking imagination seriously in education would seem to have implications for the curriculum as well as for teaching. There is not space here to try to work these out in detail (for which see Egan, 1990, esp. Ch. 9), but a few brief observations seem appropriate.

Sometimes a focus on generic capacities, such as imagination, is used to support curriculum schemes that do not follow traditional disciplinary boundaries. One can see how focussing on "thinking skills" or "teaching for thinking" or "problem-solving" or "imagination" might encourage one to focus away from the particular content of mathematics, science, history (Barrow, 1990). So "integration" of subjects, through a focus on themes or whatever, tends to be favoured by many who are sympathetic with encouraging more imaginative engagements with content. I think some part of this preference is due to an assumption that traditional ways of teaching traditional subjects are inevitably unimaginative. I think that this connection is not a necessary one and the assumption that it is can lead to throwing babies out with bath-water.

Many contemporary educationalists consider "interdisciplinary study" or "integration" of subjects important to revitalize the curriculum. I must confess that I cannot get very excited about this long-standing dispute, which has tended to be one of the grounds for distinguishing "progressive" from "traditionalist" forces. Certainly I find it hard to see why moving towards integration of subjects should help students' understanding and engagement. Equally, theme-focussed work that transcends disciplinary boundaries seems an unlikely candidate for the destroyer of civilization as we know it — as the more millenial traditionalists seem to suggest. "A bit of both" seems a reasonable compromise. While the framework does seem to make interdisciplinary or integrated units more easy to compose, as I noted at the end of the last chapter, it seems fair to conclude that a focus on imagination does not imply integration of subjects. Indeed, to echo Brian Sutton-Smith's observation: "Every subject matter requires its own 'what if' speculation, its own place in the imagination" (Sutton-Smith, 1988, p. 22).

Mary Warnock asks at the conclusion to her *Schools of Thought* (1977) what features a curriculum should have if it is to be imagination-enhancing. She identifies four features. First she argues for a curriculum in which students are given a wide choice of options. Second, she argues that students should engage in some form of specialization, which she thinks will likely "give greater play to the imagination" because it "is only by considering a thing deeply and for its own sake that one can properly begin to enjoy or understand it" (p. 157). Third, she believes that art activities are crucial because they encourage finer and more thoughtful perception and deeper emotional experience, and thus lead to the educational development of our perceptions and emotions. More arts in the curriculum, she suggests, would probably be of greater social, and educational, value than pastoral or counselling services. Relatedly, she wants students to be able to contemplate the beauty of the natural world, and learn to hear and feel "the ghostly language of the ancient earth", as Wordsworth puts it and she quotes it (p. 162). Fourth, she argues that each student needs some solitude: The imagination "works surreptitiously and quietly" (p. 162), and it is in the silent recollection and contemplation of what has been learnt or experienced that the imagination goes most effectively to work.

How far does my discussion of imagination in education imply a curriculum that would satisfy Warnock's criteria? I think I have adequately addressed the points about specialization and about the arts and nature. Her point about providing a wide choice of options is to some degree implicit in some of the principles elaborated above. A tight curriculum that seeks to coerce the imagination into energetic life seems something of a contradiction. But to be too insistent about its being contradictory would be dangerous. There have been too many cases of ferocious compulsion leading to immense imaginative achievements. Beethoven and Mozart were not enabled to achieve their great imaginative works by being offered a wide variety of options for study. But I think one has to acknowledge that a curriculum that allows students some freedom of choice is probably to be preferred to one that doesn't. I must admit I do not see compelling arguments or evidence to justify putting it any stronger than this. (Also, I suppose this point only becomes clear when we get down to details of just what kind and extent of choice one means.)

The fourth point, about solitude, I don't think I have addressed at all. Warnock thinks that some room for mental solitude can come within routine curriculum organization, and from old-fashioned teacher-directed lessons. She suggests a paradox in which a kind of boredom in school can be stimulating to the imagination. Slight boredom allows the mind to relax and wander; it allows mental freedom and solitude, as the student glazedly looks out the window or contemplates the designs on the ceiling. She notes the pervasive belief — perhaps even stronger in North America and Australia than in Great Britain — that students engaged in cooperative work, communicating and socializing even from the earliest years, is thought to be very beneficial. This pervasive belief tends to encourage conditions that are not especially hospitable to imaginative development. Clearly, cooperative activity can stimulate imaginations working together, but the importance of solitude, comfort with being alone, comfort with a kind of silence in the mind — free from incessant bombardment by talk, entertainment, radio and T.V. noise, and so on — she thinks is greatly underestimated. She wants a curriculum structure that gives significant opportunity for students' minds to range free, to think of many and diverse things as possibly being so. She is not promoting teaching that bores students, but simply making the point that sometimes such teaching can allow a desirable kind of mental freedom. If this is our aim we might be able to plan for it in our curriculum without having to resort to the kinds of teaching practices that by default allow it sometimes to occur. I think her general point here is a valuable one. How we might accommodate the curriculum to it seems open to a number of solutions. One that is consistent with the principles articulated above is to ensure that individual students can engage with an individual piece of work over a long period of time — perhaps a year — with minimal shaping pressure from teachers.

Eliminating Social Studies and Humanities

Perhaps the most radical curriculum change that seems to me to be implied by the foregoing discussion of imagination in education would be the elimination of "social studies" and, where it occurs, of "humanities" as subject-areas. The former is a mainstay of elementary and secondary curricula in the United States and Australia. The form it takes as a secondary subject in Britain and parts of Canada is rather different, and these comments are less directed at that form of it, though I think the point I will make briefly below could be elaborated to an argument for its abolition too.

The argument against social studies goes as follows. Let me begin by sketching what I see as the main curriculum components implied by the principles articulated above. There would be five major strands: Arts, Sciences, Mathematics and Logic, History, Languages (geography would be a science and computing, used pervasively, would form a part of Mathematics and Logic). I think the principles above also support a set of smaller topics, taking briefer periods of time during the day — a number of them in quarter-hour blocks. These would include Ideas, People Past and Present, The Technology of Familiar Things, The Universe, Animal and Plant Life, and Other Countries and Ways of Living. Clearly, these are neither mutually exclusive of each other or of the five major strands, but they would be approached differently, drawing differentially on some of the principles concerning imaginative engagement and stimulation. How is the omission of social studies justified?

Social studies was introduced into the curriculum in the U.S. early in this century for the particular, pressing need to use the school curriculum to socialize to what were unquestioned American norms the "huddled masses" of dozens of different countries with dozens of different languages. The pedagogical justification for social studies was given more elaborately and profoundly by John Dewey than by anyone else. He saw the purpose of social studies as central to the curriculum, intended to "humanize" other subjects by relating their content to the students' living social experience. What happened over the decades is that social studies became another distinct curriculum topic in a time-slot of its own, with a content of its own designed by social studies professors and teachers working independently from those revising mathematics, languages, science, and other curricula.

That is, Dewey's idea was to have social studies as a central integrating curriculum area which would give life and meaning to other curriculum subjects by locating them within the social lives and experience of the students. He wanted the contents of social sciences "dealt with less as sciences (less as formulated bodies of knowledge) and more in their direct subject-matter as that is found in the daily life of the social groups in which the student shares" (Dewey, 1966, p. 201). By making social studies an independent subject area this central role has been undermined. But what I have been suggesting throughout this book is an alternative way of achieving the end Dewey proposed. It is an alternative that makes social studies and humanities redundant; every subject is to be imbued with a social and human dimension.

Perhaps I might add a note about the place of history in this "imagination-enhancing" curriculum, especially as I am dispensing with social studies, into which it is yoked in much of North America and Australia, and as I have pushed its yoke-mate, geography, into the sciences. From what I have written above, it will be clear that history is to be central to this putative curriculum. It is the great story of our culture, the context we require to give anything we learn proportionate meaning. Prominent in this imaginative history curriculum during the middle-school years will be narrative, personality, event, vivid detail, human passion, experience different from students' own, the exotic and the heroic — all of them implicit in the characteristics elaborated throughout this book.

Again, in parts of North America and in Australia, where social studies and the ideas that it has carried with it are prevalent, one sees commonly asserted, as though it is too obvious to need arguing, that "the primary rationale for teaching history to school students [is] citizenship education" (Thornton, 1990, p. 58). This is an issue whose full import is too complex to deal with here, except to note the impoverished conception of history implicit in such claims. Knowledge of history does two things; it creates an intellectual dimension to our experience which we conceive of as the past, whose concomitant is that it opens up an intellectual dimension to our experience which we conceive of as the future. That is, the sense of a future which can be made different from the present — the basis for our conception of social change — is a product of the sense of history. The richer our sense of history, the fuller our understanding of the past, the better able we are to deal with social change, the better sense we can make of social experience that is constantly changing, and the better able we are to think of distinct possible futures. Now some people may mean something like this when they refer to using history for "citizenship", though, it must be said, there is no evident recognition of the psychological effects of historical understanding. Moreover, the curricula that follow from claims about history's role being "citizenship education" are typically of the crudest, most simple-mindedly utilitarian kind, prescribing content in proportion to its proximity to students' current social experience.

This head-on attack on social studies may no doubt seem rather odd following as it does the example of applying the "romantic" framework to the topic of "government". What I wanted to show in the previous chapter was that the framework can be applied to any content, and I chose a conveniently common social studies topic rather than an historical one without meaning to imply any curriculum recommendation. Teachers will no doubt have to deal with social studies topics for some time yet, despite whatever arguments I can make, and my aim here is simply to indicate how such required topics may be made more imaginatively engaging. (My perhaps eccentric and inadequately informed view of social studies is so unsympathetic that I have had difficulty imaginatively engaging the topic of "government" and so have produced a rather weak and not affectively engaging example. I do not think the resulting weakness is a defect of the framework so much as of my imagination here; I hope teachers more sympathetic with the aims of social studies might use the framework to better effect.)

Imagination and Entertainment

Whenever people write about making teaching and learning imaginatively engaging there rises up, appropriately, the objection that this can be a covert way of replacing education with entertainment. It creates images of a neuron-popping, *Sesame Street*-like, advertising-inspired hype that may have only the most marginal connection with education, and which positively undermines intensive and extensive learning. Sometimes people who promote "imagination" seem like fairground salesmen, peddling immense returns for little effort. Suspicion of such proffered bargains is entirely proper.

Appeal to imagination is not infrequently made in order to justify entertaining activities that are indeed hard to square with the purposes of education. There is obviously nothing wrong with making schooling more entertaining, but it is important to hold a clear distinction between that aim and educating. Things educational can often be entertaining, but things entertaining are not always educational — unless one holds the most flaccid conception of education wherein all experience is educational. This is not the place for distinctions worked over adequately by analytic philosophy of education, especially as my point in raising the distinction is to underline a potential danger that can follow reading the earlier material too casually. The danger is to take the principles or the framework embodying them as "motivating techniques" or as "hooks" to pull at students' attention and, once a spark of life is generated, to go back to business as usual. The point of the principles and framework is that they require the teacher to see the content as having to be taught differently. That is, it is the whole of the topic that is to be reconceived — not just a few bright bits and pieces injected into a topic otherwise left unimaginatively grasped. Also what I have been emphasizing is that topics are to be made imaginatively engaging by reconceiving the subject matter itself, not merely drawing on something extraneous to stimulate initial interest.

Interests and Abilities: Educational Clichés

Another way of considering why imagination is important to education is to examine the clichés that currently guide much educational practice. To take a very prominent example, we are told that in teaching we must "start from where the students are". This is, like many similar clichés, the result of important insights, and we would obviously be foolish to ignore it. But once we accept its importance as a guide to practice and begin to think about it carefully, the clear guidance it appears to offer becomes a little problematic. Where "are" the students of a typical class?

Most commonly the principle embedded in the cliché is used to justify selecting curriculum content that is a part of the familiar environment to which students belong, as a starting point for units or lessons. It is also used to justify trying to describe students' stage of development, ability level, relevant prior knowledge, learning styles, and so on. These can obviously be beneficial in helping to plan effective teaching. But the most common uses of the principle with regard to curriculum content and to psychological conditions are also prone to interpretations that are educationally dysfunctional. The refinements of epistemological and psychological theories are commonly reduced to claims about "where students are" that seem to ignore the fact that students have imaginations.

Unfortunately many teachers seem to have accepted uncritically certain stereotypes of students that actually get in the way of their seeing "where the students are". In the case of curriculum content, the stereotype of students' interests from which one can motivatingly start is largely restricted to the familiar content of their daily experience. In the case of psychological conditions, the stereotype of students' forms of thinking is largely restricted to descriptions of their logico-mathematical cognitive skills.

These restricting stereotypes are brought under critical scrutiny once our assessment of "where students are" takes seriously their imaginative lives. Then the notion that the most engaging content is to be found in their local environments and everyday experience looks entirely implausible, and the assumption that their logico-mathematical skills determine what they can have access to looks impoverished. This is not to suggest that there is no value in trying to assess students' cognitive skills, levels of development, learning styles and so on, nor in analyzing what features of students' local environments and daily experience can play a connecting role to new knowledge. My point is, what were once important insights can degenerate into stereotypes that begin to undermine the purposes they were originally intended to serve. The degeneration has occurred in these cases, I am suggesting, because their educational implementation has gone forward with too little, if any, attention to the characteristics of students' imaginative lives. My purpose in this book has been to reassert the importance of attending to students' imaginations and to see how taking imagination seriously might affect some of our most common educational beliefs.

The Moral Dimension

It is hard to leave a book about aspects of students' imaginative lives during the middle school years without any reference to their moral consciousness. During the years around puberty, students become increasingly aware of themselves as moral agents. It is a period of life in which awareness of the self as individual, autonomous, and social all grow together — a complexity no-one comes to terms with entirely easily. They are moving from more or less complete dependence to increasing independence; this leads to complex adjustments as they both resist the constraints of adult society while beginning to find a place within it. The power to think of the possible can clearly play an important role in this major transition. With their increasing independence and autonomy students increasingly become moral agents. Moral agency is tied in with the power to make choices. And the power to make choices is again tied in with the power to conceive of different possibilities. To realize our individuality requires our learning what is right for us among the range of possibilities open to us. The greater our imaginative power, it would seem to follow, the greater our moral autonomy. To go along with the crowd, to fit in, to do the conventional, is in part due to not *realizing* the possible alternatives open to us. (In part, of course, it has to do with other features of the personality beyond the scope of this short book, and a more powerful imagination can lead to greater wickedness no less easily than to greater good.)

While the word "moral" has appeared very rarely, if at all, hitherto in this book, I think that aspect of students' lives has not been neglected. When focussing on the means to make the lives of others meaningful to students, on humanizing knowledge, on imaginatively engaging with people's hopes, fears, and intentions, and so on, we are focussing on matters that are intricately bound up with morality. So, while there is little explicit discussion of the moral dimension, I think it is fair to observe that this discussion of students' imaginative lives rarely moves far from moral issues.

The Logic of the Heart

So there is within us something *generative*, productive, something able to conceive of impossibilities, to think of things as possibly being so, something able to *imagine* — no other word quite catches the uniqueness of what we all can experience but have great difficulty describing. We can be moved by the products of our imaginative activity, we can feel about them in painting, literature, and music, and we can respond aesthetically to them in science, mathematics, and technology. What we can imagine can thus guide our painting or our technology to generate something that makes the world closer to our heart's desire.

In the 1780s Herder observed what we might with equal accuracy observe today:

> Of all the powers of the human mind the imagination has been the least explored, probably because it is the most difficult to explore... — it seems to be not only the basic and connecting link of all the finer mental powers, but in truth the knot that ties body and mind together.
>
> (cited in McFarland, 1985, p. xiii)

Discussion of imagination draws us to consider memory, metaphor, story, and emotion. Its logic is tied to the heart no less than to the head. Let me conclude with the point I have made consistently through this book: imagination is not something we gain at the expense of rationality. Imagination must dwell within rationality if rationality is to serve human life and enrich our experience. Rationality without imagination is merely dessicated calculation, where crucial terms in the calculations are impossible to evaluate, and so such calculations go wild and fail to account for or to contribute to the richness of human life. Rationality without imagination is blind, rudderless, and as likely to destroy what is of human value as help it. In education, theories of learning, procedures for planning and managing teaching, attempts to teach "rational skills", "critical thinking", "problem-solving" or whatever, that employ conceptions of rationality deficient in imagination are at best arid and at worst damaging. Perhaps our minds are only, in Marvin Minsky's celebrated phrase, "computers made of meat", but our mental computers have the capacity to think of things as possibly being so, and this peculiar capacity, the capacity of imagination, is still so little understood that characterizing it in terms of easily grasped calculation is at this stage unwise.

We have been too long in shaking off nineteenth-century positivist notions of rationality, especially in education. Their residue is pervasive in educational research, in curricula, in professional-development programmes for teachers. One way to redress this long imbalance is to take imagination more seriously.

References

Abrams, M.H. (1958). *The mirror and the lamp: Romantic theory and the critical tradition*. New York: Norton.

Bacon, Francis. (1864-74). *Works* (eds. J. Spedding, R.L. Ellis, & D.D. Heath). London: Longmans.

Bailin, Sharon. (1988). *Achieving extraordinary ends: An essay on creativity*. Boston: Kluwer.

Barrow, Robin. (1984). *Giving teaching back to teachers: A critical introduction to curriculum theory*. Brighton: Wheatsheaf; London, Ontario: The Althouse Press.

Barrow, Robin. (1990). *Understanding skills: Thinking, feeling, and caring*. London, Ontario: The Althouse Press.

Benjamin, Walter. (1969). *Illuminations* (trans. Harry Zohn). New York: Schocken Books.

Bertoff, Ann. (1984). *Reclaiming the imagination: Philosophical perspectives for writers and teachers of writing*. Portsmouth, NH: Boynton/Cook.

Bertoff, Ann. (1990). I.A. Richards, Coleridge, and imagination. In John Willinsky (ed.), *The educational legacy of romanticism*. Waterloo, Ontario: Wilfrid Laurier University Press.

Block, Ned. (ed.) (1981). *Imagery*. Cambridge, MA: MIT Press.

Bloom, Alan. (1987). *The closing of the American mind: How higher education has failed democracy and impoverished the souls of today's students*. New York: Simon & Schuster.

Blumenberg, Hans. (1985). *Work on myth* (trans. Robert M. Wallace). Cambridge, MA: MIT Press.

Blumenberg, Hans. (1987). *The genesis of the Copernican world* (trans. Robert M. Wallace). Cambridge, MA: MIT Press.

Bowra, C.M. (1949). *Romantic imagination*. Cambridge, MA: Harvard University Press.

Bruner, Jerome. (1986). *Actual minds, possible worlds*. Cambridge, MA: Harvard University Press.

Burke, Edmund. (1967). *A philosophical inquiry into the origin of our ideas of the sublime and beautiful* (ed. J.T. Boulton). London: Routledge and Kegan Paul.

Callahan, R. (1962). *Education and the cult of efficiency*. Chicago: University of Chicago Press.

Coe, Richard (1984). *When the grass was taller*. New Haven: Yale University Press.

Coles, Robert. (1989). *The call of stories: Teaching and the moral imagination*. Boston: Houghton Mifflin.

Croce, Benedetto. (1972). *Aesthetic*. New York: Farrar.

Cullingford, Cedric. (1991). *The inner world of the school*. London: Cassell.

Descartes, René. (1917). *A discourse on method* (trans. J. Veitch). London: Dent.

Descartes, René. (1931). *The philosophical works of Descartes* (eds. and trans. E.S. Haldane, & G.R.T. Ross). Cambridge, MA: Cambridge University Press.

Dewey, John. (1966). *Democracy and education*. New York: Free Press. (First published 1916).

Dinnage, Rosemary. (1990, December). *Fragments of a remade world*. Times Literary Supplement, 22-28.

Donoghue, Denis. (1973). *Thieves of fire*. London: Faber.

Dunlop, Francis. (1988). Thinking in images. *Journal of Philosophy of Education, 22*(2).

Egan, Kieran. (1986). *Teaching as story telling: An alternative approach to teaching and curriculum in the elementary school*. London, Ontario: The Althouse Press; Chicago: University of Chicago Press, 1988; London: Routledge, 1988.

Egan, Kieran. (1988). *Primary understanding: Education in early childhood*. New York and London: Routledge.

Egan, Kieran. (1990). *Romantic understanding: The development of rationality and imagination, ages 8-15*. New York and London: Routledge.

Egan, Kieran & Nadaner, Dan. (eds.) (1988). *Imagination and education*. New York: Teachers College Press; Milton Keynes: Open University Press.

Eisner, Elliot W. (1985). *The educational imagination* (2nd edition). New York: Macmillan.

Engell, James. (1982). *The creative imagination: Enlightenment to romanticism*. Cambridge, MA: Harvard University Press.

Frye, Northrop. (1957). *Anatomy of criticism*. Princeton, NJ: Princeton University Press.

Frye, Northrop. (1963). *The educated imagination*. Toronto: Canadian Broadcasting Corporation.

Galton, Francis. (1883). *Inquiries into human faculty and its development*. London: Macmillan.

Gardner, Howard. (1985). *The mind's new science*. New York: Basic Books.

Guba, E.G., & Lincoln, Y.S. (1981). *Effective evaluation: Improving the usefulness of evaluation results through responsive and naturalistic approaches.* San Francisco: Jossey-Bass.

Halling, Steen. (1987). The imaginative constituent in interpersonal living: Empathy, illusion, and will. In Edward L. Murray (ed.), *Imagination and phenomenological psychology.* Pittsburgh, PA: Duquesne University Press.

Hammond, David. (1990). *The common play of ironic understanding.* Unpublished M.A. thesis. Montreal: McGill University.

Hanson, Karen. (1988). Prospects for the good life: Education and perceptive imagination. In K. Egan and D. Nadaner (eds.), *Imagination and education.* New York: Teachers College Press; Milton Keynes: Open University Press.

Hardy, Barbara. (1968). Towards a poetics of fiction: An approach through narrative. *Novel, 2,* 5-14.

Havelock, Eric A. (1963). *Preface to Plato.* Cambridge, MA: Harvard University Press.

Havelock, Eric A. (1986). *The muse learns to write.* New Haven: Yale University Press.

Hirsch, E.D. Jr. (1987). *Cultural literacy: What every American needs to know.* Boston: Houghton Mifflin.

Hobbes, Thomas. (1962). *Leviathan.* London: Dent. (First published 1651).

Hume, David. (1888). *A treatise of human nature* (ed. L.A. Selby-Bigge). Oxford: Oxford University Press.

Kant, Immanuel. (1952). *Critique of judgement* (trans. J.C. Meredith). Oxford: Oxford University Press.

Kearney, Richard. (1988). *The wake of imagination.* London: Hutchinson.

Kirk, Geoffrey. (1970). *Myth: Its meaning and functions in ancient and other cultures.* Cambridge: Cambridge University Press; Berkeley and Los Angeles: California University Press.

Kirkpatrick, E.A. (1957). *Imagination and its place in education.* New York: Basic Books.

Kleibard, Herbert M. (1986). *The struggle for the American curriculum: 1893-1958.* Boston: Routledge and Kegan Paul.

Koestler, Arthur. (1964). *The act of creation.* New York: Macmillan.

Kolakowski, Leszek. (1989). *The presence of myth.* Chicago: University of Chicago Press.

Kosslyn, Stephen M. (1980). *Image and mind.* Cambridge, MA: Harvard University Press.

Kosslyn, Stephen M. (1983). *Ghosts in the mind's machine: Creating and using images in the brain.* New York: Norton.

Lakoff, George, & Johnson, Mark. (1980). *Metaphors we live by.* Chicago: University of Chicago Press.

Langer, Susanne K. (1967, 1972, 1982). *Mind: An essay on human feeling.* Vols. 1, 2 & 3. Baltimore: Johns Hopkins University Press.

Le Goff, Jacques. (1986). *L'imagination mediévale.* Paris: Gallimard.

Lévi-Bruhl, Lucien. (1985). *How natives think* (trans. Lilian A. Clare; Intro. C. Scott Littleton). Princeton, NJ: Princeton University Press. (First published, 1910).

Lévi-Strauss, Claude. (1966). *The savage mind.* Chicago: University of Chicago Press.

Lindsay, P.H., & D.A. Norman. (1977). *Human information processing* (2nd ed.). New York: Academic Press.

Macaulay, David. (1973). *Cathedral: The story of its construction.* Boston: Houghton Mifflin.

Macaulay, David. (1975). *Pyramid.* Boston: Houghton Mifflin.

Macaulay, David. (1977). *Castle.* Boston: Houghton Mifflin.

MacIntyre, Alasdair. (1981). *After virtue.* Notre Dame, Indiana: University of Notre Dame Press.

Maslow, A.H. (1970). *Motivation and personality* (2nd ed.). New York: Harper and Row.

McFarland, Thomas. (1985). *Originality and imagination.* Baltimore: Johns Hopkins University Press.

Mills, Stephen. (1990). Review in the *Times Literary Supplement,* May 11-17, p. 490.

Mock, Ruth. (1971). *Education and the imagination.* London: Chatto and Windus.

Murray, Edward L. (1987). Imagination theory and phenomenological thought. In Edward L. Murray (ed.), *Imagination and phenomenological psychology.* Pittsburgh, PA: Duquesne University Press.

Novitz, David. (1987). *Knowledge, fiction and imagination.* Philadelphia: Temple University Press.

O'Neil, P.G. (1988). Teaching effectiveness: A review of the research. *Canadian Journal of Education, 13,* 1, 162-185.

Ong, Walter. (1982). *Orality and literacy.* London and New York: Methuen.

Paivio, Allan. (1965). Abstractness, imagery, and meaningfulness in paired associate learning. *Journal of Verbal Learning and Verbal Behavior, 4,* 32-38.

Paivio, Allan. (1971). *Imagery and verbal processes*. New York: Holt, Rinehart & Winston.

Pappas, Theori. (1989). *The joy of mathematics*. San Carlos, CA: Wide Word Publishing/Tetra. (Revised edition.).

Patton, Michael Quinn. (1990). *Qualitative evaluation and research methods* (2nd ed.). Newbury Park, CA: Sage.

Paz, Octavio. (1989). Imaginary gardens: A memoir. *Times Literary Supplement.* July 14-20.

Picard, Barbara Leonie. (1953). *Norse gods and heroes*. Oxford: Oxford University Press.

Polanyi, Michael. (1967). *The tacit dimension*. New York: Anchor Books.

Porter, A.C., & Brophy, J. (1988). Synthesis of research on good teaching: Insights from the work of the Institute for Research on Teaching. *Educational Leadership, 45*, 74-85.

Pylyshyn, Zenon. (1979). Imagery theory: Not mysterious — just wrong. *The Behavioral and Brain Sciences, 3*, 442-44.

Pylyshyn, Zenon. (1981). The imagery debate: Analog media versus tacit knowledge. In N. Block (ed.), *Imagery (pp. 151-206)*. Cambridge, MA: MIT Press.

Pylyshyn, Zenon. (1984). *Computation and cognition: Toward a foundation for cognitive science*. Cambridge, MA: MIT Press.

Ravitch, Diane, & Finn, Chester E., Jr. (1987). *What do our 17-year-olds know?* New York: Harper and Row.

Ricoeur, Paul. (1965). *History and truth*. Evanston: Northwestern University Press.

Ricoeur, Paul. (1978). Imagination in discourse and in action. In A. Tymieniecka (ed.), *Analecta Husserliama* (pp. 3-22), *7, .* Dordrecht: Holland.

Rorty, Richard. (1990). The dangers of over-philosophication. *Educational Theory, 40*(1), 41-44.

Rosenblatt, Louise. (1938). *Literature as exploration*. New York: Appleton-Century-Croft.

Rugg, Harold. (1963). *Imagination*. New York: Harper and Row.

Ryle, Gilbert. (1949). *The concept of mind*. London: Hutchinson.

Sartre, Jean-Paul. (1972). *The psychology of imagination*. London: Methuen.

Schubert, William H. (1986). *Curriculum: Perspective, paradigm, and possibility*. New York: Macmillan.

Shepard, Roger. (1988). The imagination of the scientist. In K. Egan and D. Nadaner (eds.), *Imagination and education*. New York: Teachers College Press; Milton Keynes: Open University Press.

Shepard, Roger, & Metzler, Jacqueline. (1971). Mental rotation of three-dimensional objects. *Science, 171,* 701-3.

Spacks, Patricia Meyer. (1981). *The adolescent idea: Myths of youth and the adult imagination.* New York: Basic Books.

Spence, Jonathan. (1984). *The memory palace of Matteo Ricci.* New York: Viking Penguin.

Springhall, John. (1986). *Coming of age: Adolescence in Britain 1860-1960.* Dublin: Gill and Macmillan.

Sutton-Smith, Brian. (1988). In search of the imagination. In K. Egan and D. Nadaner (eds.), *Imagination and education.* New York: Teachers College Press; Milton Keynes: Open University Press.

Swift, Graham. (1983). *Waterland.* London: Heinemann.

Tanner, Daniel, & Tanner, Laurel. (1980). *Curriculum development: Theory into practice* (2nd ed.). New York: Macmillan.

Thornton, Stephen J. (1990). Should we be teaching more History? *Theory and Research in Social Education,* XVIII(1).

Tyler, Ralph. (1949). *Basic principles of curriculum and instruction.* Chicago: University of Chicago Press.

Walsh, William. (1959). *The use of imagination.* London: Chatto and Windus.

Warnock, Mary. (1976). *Imagination.* London: Faber.

Warnock, Mary. (1977). *Schools of thought.* London: Faber.

Wellek, René & Warren, Austin. (1949). *Theory of literature.* New York: Harcourt Brace Jovanovich.

White, Alan R. (1990). *The language of imagination.* Oxford: Blackwell.

Willinsky, John. (ed.) (1990). *The educational legacy of Romanticism.* Waterloo, Ontario: Wilfred Laurier University Press.

Wordsworth, William. (1940-1949). *The poetical works of William Wordsworth* (eds. Ernest de Selincourt and Helen Darbishire), 5 vols. Oxford: Clarendon Press.

Yates, Frances. (1966). *The art of memory.* Chicago: University of Chicago Press.

Index

ABRAMS, M.H., 26, 169n
Addison, Joseph, 19
Affect, 21, 32, 40, 69-72, 87, 105, 158
Affective teaching, 70, 87, 108, 109, 113
Archetype, 75, 76
Aristotle, 15-18, 35
Awe, 75, 78-80, 110, 130, 139, 140, 147

BACON, FRANCIS, 19, 169n
Bailin, Sharon, 37, 169n
Barrow, Robin, 1, 3, 31, 37, 157, 169n
Behaviourism, 34, 91
Benjamin, Walter, 55, 169n
Bertoff, Ann, 29, 169n
Block, Ned, 35, 169n
Bloom, Alan, 53, 169n
Blumenberg, Hans, 10, 169n
Brophy, J., 1, 173n
Bruner, Jerome, 51, 169n
Burke, Edmond, 20, 169n

CALLAHAN, R., 91, 169n
Coe, Richard, 25, 169n
Coleridge, Samuel Taylor, 22-24, 27, 29, 36, 58
Coles, Robert, 55, 65, 170n
Collecting, 85
Commenius, 51
Concepts, 40, 115-118
Conventional thinking, 46-49, 51
Copernicus, 24
Creativity, 61, 62
Croce, Benedetto, 15, 170n
Cullingford, Cedric, 64, 170n
Curriculum, 156-162

DAYDREAMING, 48, 58, 159
Democracy, 135, 136, 140, 141
Descartes, René, 18, 19, 22, 39, 170n
Detail, study of, 84-86, 106, 107, 111, 141
Dewey, John, 5, 46, 47, 65, 91, 105, 160, 161, 170n
Diaries, 80
Disciplines, 59, 60, 157-162
Donoghue, Denis, 13, 170n

EFFECTIVE TEACHING, 1, Chs. 4, 5, and 6 *passim*, 154-156
Einstein, Albert, 62
Eisner, Elliot W., 101, 150, 170n
Emotion, 4, 9-12, 51, 52, 55, 158. *See also* Affect
Empirical research, 68, 69, 88, 167
Engell, James, 20, 170n
Enlightenment, The, 18-22
Entertainment, 162, 163
Eratosthenes, 117, 121-124
Evaluation, 100-102, 124, 125, 132, 133, 143, 144, 149, 150
Extremes of human experience, 72-75, 86
Extremes of reality, 72-75, 109, 110

FACTORIES, as influence on schools, 153, 154
Fancy, 19, 23
Fiction, 54-56
Finn, Charles E. Jr., 53, 173n
Framework for planning, 94
Freedom, 57-59
Freud, Sigmund, 41
Frye, Northrop, 56, 63, 64, 70, 170n

GALTON, FRANCIS, 33, 39, 170n
Gardner, Howard, 34, 35, 170n

Geometry, 120-125
Green, Maxine, 3
Guba, E.G., 102, 143, 150, 171n
Guided imagery, 61, 62

HALLING, STEEN, 31, 33, 171n
Hammond, David, 42, 171n
Hanson, Karen, 58, 171n
Hardy, Barbara, 64, 171n
Herder, Johann Gottfried, 22, 166
Heroism, 80-82, 110, 113
Heroes, 80-82, 140
Hirsch, E.D. Jr., 48, 53, 171n
History, in the curriculum, 161,
    162
Hobbes, Thomas, 17, 171n
Hobbies, 85
Hughes, Ted, 3, 61, 171n
Humanities, in the curriculum,
    159-162
Humanizing knowledge, 86, 87,
    105, 106, 112, 121, 130, 160
Hume, David, 20-22, 26, 31, 38,
    39, 69, 171n
Husserl, Edmund, 28

IDEALISM, 82-84, 111
Ideals, 111, 131, 148
Ignorance, 47, 52, 155
Images/Imagery, 3, 4, 11 ,17,
    28-36, 115-118
    affective, 104, 113, 115-118,
    126
    scannable, 31, 32, 35, 36
Imaging, 33-36
Imagination,
    ancient and medieval, 12-18
    as creative, 23-26, 36
    as intentional, 23, 28, 38
    as mimesis, 14, 15, 17
    as perception, 15, 17
    characteristics of adolescents',
    67-89
    educational importance of,
    45-65

history of, 9-43
in *The Enlightenment*, 18-22
primary/secondary, 22, 23
psychological views of, 33-36
reproductive/generative uses
    of, 15, 24, 36
variety of meanings, 2, 9
Imaginativeness, 1, 30, 31, 36,
    37, 43
Industrial Revolution, 26
Integration, of subject areas, 152,
    157, 161
Interests, students', 163-165
"Intimations of Immortality", 25

JOHNSON, MARK, 62, 172n
Justice, 54-57

KANT, IMMANUEL, 20-24, 31,
    171n
Kearney, Richard, 12, 15, 18, 26,
    28, 171n
Keats, John, 26
Kirk, Geoffrey, 10, 171n
Kliebard, Herbert M., 91, 171n
Koestler, Arthur, 37, 171n
Kolakowski, Leszek, 62, 171n
Kosslyn, Stephen M., 34, 35, 62,
    171n, 172n

LAKOFF, GEORGE, 62, 172n
Langer, Susanne K., 62, 172n
Language arts, 144-150
Learning, 5, 49-52
    imaginative, 53
    influence of technology on,
    86, 87
    principles, 107-112
Le Goff, Jacques, 17, 172n
Lesson planning, 92, Chs. 4, 5,
    and 6 *passim*, 154
Lincoln, Y.S., 102, 143, 150, 171n
Lindsay, P.H., 35, 172n
Literacy, 49, 71
Literature, in the curriculum, 117

Logico-mathematical thinking, 5,
  6, 46, 64, 164

MACAULAY, DAVID, 117,
  172n
MacIntyre, Alasdair, 54, 64, 70,
  172n
Malebranche, Nicholas, 19
Maslow, A.H., 129, 172n
Matthews, Gareth, 3
McFarland, Thomas, 18, 22, 166,
  172n
Meaning, construction of, 21, 29,
  50, 63, 75, 76, 87
Memorization, 52-54, 155
Memory, 3, 10-12, 35, 50, 52-54,
  155
Mirandola, Pico della, 18, 172n
Metaphor, 3, 4, 40, 63, 116
Metzler, Jacqueline, 35, 174n
Mill, John Stuart, 32
Mimesis, 14, 24
Mock, Ruth, 59, 172n
Moral consciousness, 165, 166
Murray, Edward L., 36, 172n
Myth, 9-11

NADANER, D., 2, 170n
Narrative, 40, 54, 62-65, 108,
  126-129, 137, 145-148, 152,
  161. *See also* Story
Neo-conservatives, 53
Norman, D.A., 35
Norse mythology, 144-149
Novitz, David, 27, 172n

OBJECTIVE KNOWLEDGE,
  59-61
O'Neil, P.G., 1, 172n
Originality, 36, 61, 62

PASSION, 21. *See also* Affect
Paivio, Allan, 34, 35, 172n, 173n
Pappas, Theori, 125, 173n

Patton, Michael Quinn, 102, 143,
  173n
Paz, Octavio, 26, 173n
Perception, 3, 28, 38
Picard, Barbara Leonie, 147, 173n
Phantasma, 16
Plato, 14-18, 46, 47, 56, 115
  Platonic curriculum, 15
Plot, 71, 75, 76
Polanyi, Michael, 60, 173n
Porter, A.C., 1, 173n
Prigogine, Elya, 33
Prometheus, 13, 14, 23
Psychology/Psychological
  Research, 33-36
Pylyshyn, Zenon, 35, 36, 173n

RATIONALISM, 19
Rationality, 10, 42, 43, 63,
  115-118, 166, 167
Ravitch, Diane, 53, 173n
Reason, 14-19, 25, 42, 62, 63
Revolt, 82-84, 111, 131, 140, 141
Richards, I.A., 29
Ricoeur, Paul, 30, 33, 173n
Romance, 75-80, 110, 130, 140,
  147
Rousseau, Jean-Jacques, 46, 47
Ryle, Gilbert, 27, 29, 173n

SARTRE, JEAN-PAUL, 27-31,
  38, 40, 58, 70, 173n
Schubert, William H., 102, 173n
Sense making, 22
Shepard, Roger, 3, 32, 34, 35,
  40, 62, 116, 173n, 174n
Social studies, 104, 133, 159-162
Social virtues, 54-57
Solitude, educational importance
  of, 158, 159
Spacks, Patricia Meyer, 82, 174n
Specialization, 158
Spence, Jonathan, 11, 174n
Springhall, John, 83, 174n
St. Augustine, 16

St. Bonaventure, 16
St. Thomas Aquinas, 17
Story, 11, 54, 63, 70, 108, 161.
 See also Narrative
Summa Theologica, 17
Sublime, 21
Sutton-Smith, Brian, 3, 30, 62,
 70, 157, 174n
Swift, Graham, 102, 174n

TANNER, DANIEL , 91, 174n
Tanner, Laurel, 91, 174n
Teacher-education, 114-118,
 154, 167
Teachers' role, 113, 119, 154-156
"Teen-romances", 79, 88
Textbooks, structure of, 84, 86,
 151
Thornton, Stephen J., 161, 174n
Tolerance, 54-57
Transcendent qualities, 80-82,
 95, 110, 120, 125, 126,
 134-136, 144, 145, 151
Trees, 125-133
Tyler, Ralph, 91, 174n

UNIT PLANNING, 92, Chs. 4
 and 5 *passim*, 154

VISUALIZATION, 29, 61, 62

WARNOCK, MARY, 2, 5, 21,
 27, 31, 32, 38, 41, 51, 157-159,
 174n
Warren, Austin, 30, 174n
Watson, John B., 34
Wellek, René, 30, 174n
White, Alan R., 4, 16, 19, 22,
 26-31, 35, 37, 39, 41, 42, 70,
 174n
Whitehead, A.N., 48
Wittgenstein, Ludwig, 27, 29, 38
Wonder, 21, 75-80, 110, 130,
 140, 147

Wordsworth, William, 24, 25, 27,
 42, 76, 158, 174n
Writing. *See* Literacy

YATES, FRANCES, 11, 174n
Yetser, 12, 13

?Phantasm or ?
 phantasma ,